Go to the Pound and Get a Dog —
Then Learn to Fly an Airplane

Life's Lessons
Acquired by a Country Lawyer
From the Courthouse Square
to the Supreme Court

H. Graham Swafford Jr.
Jasper, Tennessee

For Sharon, who took a big chance
on a boy from South Pittsurg, Tenn.
I hope I was worth it.

Go to the Pound and Get a Dog —
Then Learn to Fly an Airplane

ISBN: 978-0-692-34563-4

Additional copies of this book may be ordered from McKendree United Methodist Church, PO Box 176, Jasper, TN 37347; mckendreejasper@ bellsouth.net; or 423-942-3888.

Introduction

For years I have contemplated writing a book. I never got around to it. Perhaps I was deluding myself when I thought I had a great book in me. Since the day I got out of law school, I have been fortunate if not blessed to have clients hire me to represent them as their attorney. Words cannot express my gratitude to these clients who have afforded me a good life, not to mention freedom to express my views and point out the obvious.

The practice of law continues to do well; however, several years ago, I was faced with a situation where I had a lot of time on my hands.

Psychologically, I got into a ditch — possibly a form of depression.

I earnestly searched and prayed for an answer. No answer came. When all else failed, I decided to go out and get a dog and learn to fly an airplane.

On the inside cover of my book you will see a portrait of my dog Sassy, a/k/a Dolly Madison, painted by my good friend, Jenny LeFone* of Memphis, Tenn.

I got my private pilot's license on July 18, 2011. I am currently working on my instrument rating. Sassy is doing well and enjoys flying with me.

This book represents lessons I have learned practicing law 35 years on the courthouse square in Jasper, Tenn. The book also includes the life lessons of 23 friends.

I would like to express my appreciation to those friends who have contributed. The lessons of my friends will be sprinkled through my book.

I will try to keep each lesson short and pointed. Some of my lessons might impress you with my brilliance and insight; some lessons will be funny; and some lessons sad. I hope some lessons provoke thought. The lessons cover a variety of topics.

You will probably disagree with some of my lessons or the lessons of my friends. Some lessons will be of no effect or value. Hopefully, some lessons will leave an impression.

If all else fails, I hope you are entertained and depart with some "quotable quotes."

After reading my book or life lessons, you might conclude in my old age I have become an eccentric "old fart" to which I offer no defense.

I am dedicating this book to my wife Sharon. Sharon married me two weeks before I started law school. Sharon took a big chance on a boy from South Pittsburg, Tenn. I hope I was worth it.

I would like to recognize my parents, Claude and Howard Swafford, and my sister, Claudia Swafford Haltom. Both of my parents and my sister are lawyers. Growing up in South Pittsburg, Tenn., was a real education. I have always felt the greatest compliment I can give parents is the fact that my sister and I have never had a confrontatory conversation.

I would like to recognize my in-laws, Jean and Pat Carson, and my sister in-law, Patty Carson Bowlin. Several years ago, Sharon and I got into a roaring argument which was not my fault. Pat Carson sided with me — *top that*! I could not ask for better in-laws.

I would like to recognize my son, Graham Swafford III and his wife, Andrea, and my daughter, Shelton Swafford Chambers and her husband, Patrick. Kennedy Marie Swafford arrived November 11, 2011 to much fanfare. Carson Mae Chambers was introduced to an awaiting world on April 02, 2012.

Last, but not least, but maybe more important, I would like to express my appreciation for my faithful secretary Brandy Pruitt. In the legal business, it is more important to have a good, faithful secretary than it is to be brilliant. Brandy is a good one.

I predict my death sometime within the next 35 years. The only thing I care about is where I spend eternity and how my children and grandchildren remember me.

I have high hopes of selling my book with profits and contributions going directly to the McKendree United Methodist Church, Highway 150, Jasper, Tenn. 37347, for the purpose of funding, engineering and constructing a Family Life Center. I ask my readers not to be bashful about ordering extra copies and telling their friends to buy multiple copies not to mention making a contribution to McKendree United Methodist Church. If nobody buys my book, any money received will go to the church for unrestricted use. We need to fix the parking lot. I will then continue my search for an answer.

I hope you enjoy my book.

Graham Swafford
Jasper, Tenn.

If you want a hand-painted portrait of your dog, give my friend Jenny a call. She will give you a great deal.

Sassy Swafford
(a/k/a Dolly Madison)
Portrait by Jenny LeFone, Memphis

Graham Swafford, standing in front of his airplane.

Graham Swafford, standing
before the Sixth Circuit Court
of Appeals in Cincinnati before
oral arguments.

The author's son, Howard Graham Swafford III.

Graham and his daughter, Shelton Swafford Chambers.

Contents

"*If you want a friend in Washington get a dog.*"
— *Harry S. Truman*

"*If you pick up a starving dog, and make him prosperous, he will not bite you. This is the principal difference between a dog and a man.*"
— *Mark Twain*

"*Heaven goes by favor; if it went by merit, you would stay out and your dog would go in.*"
— *Mark Twain*

"*You learn in this business: if you want a friend, get a dog.*"
— *Carl Icahn*

A Mother's Undying Love
By Graham Swafford

*I*n the late 1930s, one of South Pittsburg, Tennessee's, most prominent ladies found herself pregnant.

This was not her first pregnancy or the family's first child.

This family was situated such that they enjoyed all the benefits offered by medical science regardless of the costs.

Early on in the pregnancy, the family was told by the treating physicians there would be complications and this would be a dangerous pregnancy. The life of the child, and particularly the mother's life, would be at a huge risk. The mother promptly told the doctors she would carry this child, regardless of the risk.

> *The mother declared... 'This is my baby.'*

Time went on and the doctors repeatedly stressed how extremely dangerous this pregnancy was to all concerned especially the mother, trying to get the family to agree that the mother should not carry this child to full term. There were tremendous risks particularly to the young mother. Without hesitation, the mother declared that she would carry this child to delivery date, stating "this is my baby."

After a difficult delivery, the mother gave birth to a healthy, not to mention a rather precocious child. The young mother miraculously lived to tell the story.

The mother's name was Mary Agnes Riggle Gentry. The child was named James Lee Gentry Jr., better known as Jim Gentry. This child grew up to become the longest running and possibly most successful General Motors dealers in the state of Tennessee.

<u>LIFE'S LESSON:</u>
A mother's undying love can conquer all.

Katherine Miller
or
What I Learned in the Third Grade
By Graham Swafford

*I*n the fall of 1959, I found myself in Miss Katherine Miller's third grade class at South Pittsburg Elementary School along with much of South Pittsburg's third grade proper society — Camille Ryan, Mary Faye Killian, Margaret Ann Braden and Bob Hill, just to name a few. South Pittsburg Elementary School was straight out of the movies. The principal at South Pittsburg Elementary School was a fellow by the name of Paul Braden. Paul Braden was a tall, partially bald fellow and can best be described as a cross between a U.S. district judge and English royalty. Professor Braden's wife was the music teacher. All I can remember about the music classes was Mrs. Braden always admonishing us to "sing louder."

We hear a lot about discipline problems in schools today. Discipline was not an issue at South Pittsburg Elementary School.

Paul Braden had a memorable faculty at South Pittsburg Elementary School. Over 50 years later, I still remember Mrs. Margaret Lewis, Miss Gertrude Michael, Mrs. Jasper Dallas Anderson, Ms. Fitzgerald, Mrs. Johnnie Hewgley, Mrs. Allie Jane Raulston, Mrs. Ruby Barnes, Mrs. Ruth Hargis, Mrs. Lovell, Mrs. Burrows and Mrs. Edna Nation. The faculty at South Pittsburg Elementary was also straight out of central casting from a Hollywood classic. Looking back on the experience, Paul Braden ran the type of public institution that the well-heeled now spend thousands a year on for private schools. South Pittsburg Elementary School was *that* good.

The janitor was a fellow by the name of Jeff Peoples. Mr. Peoples was always running up and down the hall with a wide-faced push broom. Mr. Peoples was at school early and late. South Pittsburg Elementary was so clean you could eat off the floor.

We read a lot about security in public schools today. Mr. Braden had a secretary named Mrs. Foutch who had an ever-watchful eye on the front door. Nobody gave security much thought with Mrs. Foutch and Mr. Braden in charge.

I would be remiss if I did not mention Elizabeth Hackworth, who was the librarian. A fair statement is that I was not the greatest scholar that ever matriculated through South Pittsburg Elementary School. I had a hard time paying attention. I was a poor math student. I just could not sit still for more than 30 seconds. Mrs. Hackworth presided over a library that had the first carpet in a school library in the state of Tennessee. I remember going to the library and sitting on the carpeted floor and learning to read. I loved the library. I loved reading. I may not have been much of a student, but I learned to read quickly. I could read a book in a day. Learning to read made all the difference in the world.

Paul Braden "ran the show" and was the total boss! There was no debate or discussion. If the president of the United States, the Pope, the chairman of the Federal Reserve, majority leader of the Senate, not to mention the Divine all showed up at the front door at South Pittsburg Elementary School they would have taken their marching orders from Professor Braden after being scoped out by Mrs. Foutch. Life was just that simple. There was no discussion.

We hear a lot about discipline problems in schools today. Discipline was not an issue at South Pittsburg Elementary School. The Hammond boys, a memorable group who lived just across from my family, told me that Mr. Braden had an electric paddle and if you were ever paddled, Mr. Braden's electric paddle was so painful that "at the end" you would have a bird egg in your hair. I am not sure where the bird egg comes from but that is what Gary Hammond told me so it must have been true.

> *Life did not remain wonderful.*

Judge Thomas W. Graham, who later went on to fame and fortune as a circuit judge, told me the electric paddle was kept in the back room. Judge Graham always seems to have inside knowledge.

In addition to "running the show" and "being the boss," Paul Braden had an ever present "watchful eye." We don't hear about oversight and responsibility in today's world. In particular, today in Marion County, Tenn., if egregious/in your face improper conduct is going on, proper society (not to mention all public officials) plead feigned ignorance. One can but speculate whether they are stupid, incompetent, blind or just spineless.

Paul Braden did not come up short in the watchful eye or oversight department nor was he stupid, incompetent, blind or spineless. I remember one Saturday I was on Holly Avenue in South Pittsburg, and I heard the fire truck and the police sirens. Nothing is more exciting for an 8-year-old than a good fire. When the fire truck and the squad cars blazed past I immediately hopped on my bicycle and was in "hot pursuit" to view or hopefully participate in all of the excitement. I loved it! It was a wonderful day! I am of the opinion all sane people are attracted to fire trucks and whaling police/squad cars.

Life did not remain wonderful. When Monday morning arrived, at South Pittsburg Elementary School, Mr. Braden's voice boomed over the school intercom first thing in the morning announcing there would be an immediate school assembly — everybody was required to attend. Up until that moment I always enjoyed school assemblies, but quickly, I realized I was in real trouble — I mean serious trouble! In front of the entire school, Mr. Braden announced that there had been a big fire in the community on Saturday and there was a "certain" student who had followed the fire truck, creating untold danger to the safety and welfare of all South Pittsburg, Tenn. Mr. Braden admonished the entire school that chasing fire trucks should never happen again and *would not* happen again. It was apparent to the whole world that I was the guilty soul. The entire school stared at me. Mr. Braden then made it crystal clear that a price would be paid "if it ever happened again."

I fell for the 'special privilege' speech every time!

So, let me bring you back to the third grade:

My teacher in the third grade was a spinster by the name of Katherine Miller, who was also out of Hollywood central casting. If Miss Miller weighed more than 90 pounds, I would be surprised. Miss Miller suffered from childhood polio which limited her ability to walk. To this day, I admiringly remember Miss Miller struggling down the hall with grim determination. There was never an excuse or apology. Miss Miller was there to "do the job" and it was done in a superior fashion.

Over 50 years later I remember that Miss Miller would, with regularity, come into the classroom and pick up a pencil. Miss Miller would then peck on her desk and say, "Students, students, attention … I have an announcement." After repeating this phrase three times, the whole class would literally be transfixed. Miss Miller would then announce with total "world coming to an end" solemnity: "Students, I would like to announce that we are going to have a special privilege."

I fell for the "special privilege" speech every time! I mean *every* time, without exception.

Every time Miss Miller would announce we were going to have a "special privilege" I anticipated she was getting ready to tell us we were going to the Super Bowl or Disneyland. Words cannot express my gullible excitement. Words cannot express how hyped Miss Miller got me. The "special privilege" never turned out to be anything more than putting up the flag or picking up trash outside, etc. Nevertheless, I always fell for Miss Miller's hype, enthusiasm and determination every time.

Fifty years later, I am reminded of my unrestrained excitement when Miss

Miller would announce, "Students, I would like to announce a special privilege."

LIFE'S LESSON:

What I Learned in the third grade at South Pittsburg Elementary School: Hype, enthusiasm, grim determination and being on the job with serious intent will leave a big impression — enough to last more than 50 years.

*Note: There is not a doubt in my mind that Mrs. Hackworth and Miss Miller are looking down at me. I would like to convey to them my appreciation. I would like to show Mrs. Hackworth my Kindle. I still love to read. I would hope Mrs. Hackworth and Miss Miller convey to Professor and Mrs. Braden that Little Graham Swafford (of South Pittsburg's third grade class in 1959) still chases fire trucks and squad cars and has no intention of ever stopping — never! Sorry Mr. Braden — some habits cannot be broken!

James Madison, Al Gore Jr. and the Importance of 'Keeping Your Base'

By Graham Swafford

*T*he following is a political lesson from facts that will be debated by scholars and those interested in politics for centuries.

James Madison was the fourth president of the United States of America. James Madison was small and so painfully shy that when he went to parties he would stand in the corner and cringe.

James Madison wrote the Bill of Rights which, in my modest opinion, is more important than the Constitution, Declaration of Independence or anything else ever written except the Holy Bible. James Madison was a genius.

In today's world of television, media, and hype, James Madison could not be elected to anything. Genius stands for nothing. In today's world, charm, television, spin, public relations, hype, not to mention a well-funded campaign derived from special interests and associated wack-os stand for everything.

James Madison married Dolly Madison. Dolly was good looking, personable, full-bodied (if you know what I mean) and was, by all accounts, great company.

My guess is that James Madison and Dolly Madison were an odd couple. In my view, Dolly recognized a genius. I would not know, but I guess Dolly did not marry James Madison for his raw, toe-curling, sex appeal. Dolly married Madison for the singular reason that she recognized genius.

I have always liked Dolly Madison. I nicknamed my dog "Dolly Madison." In my view, James Madison would have never been president of the United States of America had it not been for Dolly.

With all the above background, we fast forward 200 years. On January 20, 1993, Al Gore Jr. of Carthage, Tenn., became the 45th vice-president of the United States of America. Intellectually, Gore reminded me of Madison — smarter than the rest and a man with a vision.

Notwithstanding my Republican pedigree, which includes two grandfathers on both my mother and father's sides, who were officers in Mr. Lincoln's Army, I always admired Al Gore Jr.

Gore's father was one of the few southern Democrats who voted for the Civil Rights Act — that took guts!

While I have never been one to pander in juicy entertaining gossip, I can say Al Gore and his family had what I felt an enviable, if not superior, reputation.

Simply stated, I admired the way Albert Gore Sr. and wife Polly, and their son, Al Gore Jr. and his wife Tipper, and their families conducted themselves. I have been told that Al Gore Jr. is a personable fellow, however I was never impressed with his charm. I really liked Gore's wife, Tipper.

But getting down to the bottom line — I thought Al Gore Jr. was brilliant and far-sighted, but perhaps a little wound up.

In today's world of television, media, and hype, James Madison could not be elected to anything. Genius stands for nothing.

Like I said before, Al Gore Jr. reminds me of Madison — a real serious fellow who not only thinks, but recognizes the obvious.

In 2001, Al Gore Jr. ran for president of the United States of America and won the popular vote by 500,000 votes. Gore did not become president because he lost the electoral college vote. In simple layman's terms, Al Gore Jr. lost the presidency of the United States of America for one singular reason — he "lost the state of Tennessee," which is his home state and his original base. It is that simple. In his previous Tennessee elections, he had repeatedly beat his Republican opposition two to one. It was never close.

Al Gore Jr. lost Tennessee because he lost the core vote that had supported both he and his father over the years. Gore lost his base!

I don't mean to sound like a prophet but "I saw it coming." Not only did everybody have an Al Gore Jr. story but particularly the "old line Democrats" were the most irritated at Al Gore Jr. In my opinion, the "yellow dogs" laid down on him.

I am of the opinion that much of the Clinton administration's success was because of the fact that Al Gore Jr. was providing adult supervision along with intelligence. An argument could be made that if Al Gore had been elected president of the United States of America we would not be bogged down in Afghanistan, we would not be running massive deficits, and we would be addressing the disastrous consequences our children will face with global warming.

LIFE'S LESSON:

In politics, brilliance is not necessary.

In politics, the ability to maintain and sustain one's base is critically important.

If a politician does not assiduously care for, feed and maintain his or her base in a non-condescending manner (at all costs) sooner, if not later, the politician will pay the price.

---

*Note: The price Al Gore Jr. paid for ignoring this lesson was the presidency of the United States. In my opinion Al Gore Jr. was exceptionally qualified to be president.

The Importance of Discipline

By Jimmy and Brenda Wigfall
South Pittsburg, Tenn.

*I*n 1965, I entered the eighth grade at South Pittsburg High School when McReynolds High School (formerly an all-black school) burned to the ground. Some say it was with a flick of a match. After the fire, McReynolds High School and South Pittsburg High School were integrated.

Before I began at South Pittsburg High School, to say I was undisciplined would be an understatement. I had no self-control. I would come and go as I pleased.

But at South Pittsburg High School, life was different. Somebody had an eye on me all the time. If I disappeared somebody would be after me.

Fifty years later, I still remember the discipline I received beginning in the eighth grade at South Pittsburg High School. The discipline made all the difference and changed my life.

> *The discipline made all the difference and changed my life.*

I remember the lectures from Mr. Beene about getting my homework done. I remember the lectures about showing up on time. I remember lectures about discipline and hard work. I remember Professor Beene's lectures to this day.

I remember simple expressions from people who offered me assistance making sure I had tennis shoes to play basketball in, etc. I remember the discipline of the 1969 football team when we won the state championship. I remember how it felt to know that we were better than anybody anywhere.

Over the years, that discipline I learned changed my life. I have been married to Brenda Wigfall for 40 years. We have a daughter and a grandchild. Nothing has been more important than the fact that as a young man I learned the importance of discipline and there were people that cared about me. Words cannot express the gratitude for the lessons I learned beginning in the eighth grade at South Pittsburg High School.

<u>LIFE'S LESSON:</u>
Learning self-discipline and that people care can make all the difference.

Brown Dog and Men Who Beat Women

By Graham Swafford

*G*rowing up on Contour Avenue in South Pittsburg, Tenn., was a great experience. Our next door neighbors were Chick and Ali Jane Raulston along with their daughters, Lynn, Jody and Dava Jane. The Hammonds (and later the Woodfins) lived across from us. The Hamptons lived across from us. The Hills lived two houses down. Growing up in this environment was safe and secure, not to mention exciting.

Over the years, my sister, Claudia, and I always had a dog. One time we had a dog named "Brown Dog." For those who might be curious, Brown Dog was … *brown.*

> *For those who might be curious, Brown Dog was …* **brown.**

Brown Dog was one of the most memorable dogs I have ever known. Brown Dog had charm and was just a likeable dog.

Brown Dog enjoyed traveling with the Swaffords. When the Swaffords would get in the car, Brown Dog would hop right in the car with us.

When we left town, Brown Dog would chase us across town and follow us all the way to the top of what was formerly McReynolds High School hill, staying up with us all the way until we physically left South Pittsburg. I don't think a Greyhound could have run as fast. It was sort of touching.

I don't mean to brag about the dog Claudia and I owned, but 50 years later I can say with absolute certainty that Brown Dog was the most talented car-chasing dog the world has ever known. Brown Dog was so talented that he could see a car coming from a distance, approach the car by charging the car head on and as the car went by, Brown Dog could bite the moving tire as it drove by barking all along. Can anybody top that? It was an impressive display of world class talent all exhibited in South Pittsburg, Tenn. You had to see it to believe it! Claudia and I will never forget Brown Dog.

Brown Dog was such a charming dog that he got all the other dogs in the neighborhood to chase cars. Specifically, Brown Dog got a couple of the Hamptons' dogs killed. I always wondered why the Hamptons did not get mad at the Swaffords for letting our dog get their dogs killed.

Having said all this about Brown Dog, I bring you to my point. What I've learned from practicing law for 35 years with literally hundreds, if not thousands, of domestic and assault cases is something I learned first from Brown Dog. There are some habits that simply cannot be broken. We loved Brown Dog. We tried to get Brown Dog to stop chasing cars — like that was going to happen! We would scold Brown Dog. We would whip Brown Dog. We would do everything to get Brown Dog to quit chasing cars — all to no avail!

Likewise, there are some habits that humans have that cannot be broken.

LIFE'S LESSON:

I have practiced law for about 35 years. The lesson from Brown Dog is "Men who beat women are like dogs that chase cars. They are creatures of habit and some habits cannot be broken."

Ms. Juanita

By Jane Coe Wilson Dawkins
South Pittsburg, Tenn.

To say that my family entertained me much of my life is probably an understatement, especially when it comes to my mother. I once heard her best friend, Marguerite White, refer to her as "the funniest white woman in South Pittsburg, Tenn." I don't know about that, but she had a great way of invoking wisdom in her wonderfully entertaining humor.

To give you a little background, Eva Juanita Brown Wilson was born during the Great Depression. Her father, Walter Brown, was fortunate to have a job at the newly opened Penn-Dixie Cement Plant. The family even had an automobile, which was rare in their neighborhood in the 1920s. At the age of five, she lost her father to cancer, leaving 6-year-old brother, Ivan, her mom and herself alone. Her mom remarried, had two more babies and divorced. Like many older children during that time, Juanita was forced to withdraw from public school to serve as housekeeper and babysitter of the younger children while her mom sewed, raised chickens and worked other odd jobs.

> *She so often said 'an education is something no one can ever take away from you.'*

In 1941, at the age of 17, Juanita met and married 18-year-old Joe Ray Wilson from Bridgeport, Alabama. Their first year of marriage was cut short with the bombing of Pearl Harbor and Joe Ray's call to the U.S. Army to serve in Europe during World War II.

Their first child, Mickey Joe, was born in 1946. He was named after comedic movie star Mickey Rooney, who had entertained the troops many times during World War II. Joe Ray had remained active in the National Guard and was called back to active duty to serve in the Korean War. After his return and the establishing of an insurance and loan business, they had a second child, Jane Coe.

Joe Ray was described by many as being "bigger than life." He became a successful businessman through insurance, banking, farming and "horse-trading" stock, property, livestock, etc. He was active in church, the community and served on boards throughout Tennessee. Juanita was a good supportive wife, mother and homemaker. She was a great cook and had what you could call "the gift of hospitality." She could entertain kings, congressmen, revival preachers, in-laws, outlaws, 5-year-olds or teenagers at the drop of a hat and make them feel immediately at home and wanting to come back again. She did not, however, fade in the shadows of such a public and dynamic husband. She had her own agendas, opinions, goals, expectations of her children and community interests — particularly in the schools. Because of her early childhood circumstances where she couldn't go very far in school, she thought every child should have (and take) the opportunity to finish high school and beyond and worked hard through the PTA and the local schools to make that happen. She so often said, "an education is something no one can ever take away from you."

Truth is, Mama was the best natural athlete in the family. She was a good bowler, played golf, croquette, etc. We knew it was summertime when she would put up a new badminton net (and break a switch and put it on top of the fridge). She loved football and never missed a South Pittsburg Pirate Game, which brings us to one of the most memorable "life lesson" true stories. This was even recanted at her funeral.

Back before experts told us you had to eat pasta before an athletic event, Ms. Juanita used to cook for Mickey and about five other players on Friday afternoons before the Pirate football games. She would cook big roasts, chicken, potatoes, cornbread and would always include a pot of pinto beans.

One particular young man ate in our home often. His mom had moved away and he stayed behind and lived with friends so he could finish school and play football. His name was Dewey. Everyone called him Admiral Dewey. One Friday afternoon "pre-game meal," he filled up his plate with meat, bread and beans and sat down at the table. Typical teenage boy trying to be cute and get a rise out of the cook, he says, "Ms. Juanita, why do you feed us pinto beans every week before the game?" With meat fork in hand standing in front of the stove, Ms. Juanita turns around quickly and responds, "Because, boys, I don't want you to run out of gas in the fourth quarter!"

Oh, the wisdom she bestowed on those boys that day. The team went on to have a great season and was invited to play in the Civitan Bowl at Tennessee Tech. Ms. Juanita helped organize a parade of fans who decorated their cars with orange and black crepe paper and signs and traveled to Cookeville in a caravan to see their Pirates, who followed Ms. Juanita's advice and did not "run out of gas in the fourth quarter."

I think she would be happy to know that her granddaughter is a lawyer, her grandson is a teacher and coaches her South Pittsburg Pirates, and there is an academic scholarship given in her name to a deserving senior each year.

LIFE'S LESSON:

Ms. Juanita passed on many words of advice and life lessons. Just to name a few:

Always wear clean underwear.

Always carry a handkerchief.

Never have hemorrhoid surgery.

You have to suffer to be pretty.

Feed a dog well at home and he will not stray.

If it doesn't fit ... force it.

If duct tape or a band aid won't fix it ... it can't be fixed.

Learn to play the piano — You'll always be the life of the party.

Good manners go a long way.

Drinking

By Graham Swafford

*N*o respectable, self-help, inspirational book would be complete without some drinking advice.

I have no statistics, but it seems like my generation does not drink like previous generations. I know my generation has been accused of being a little wild at times, but we are tame compared to older lawyers. Specifically, those older fellows (some refer to as the Greatest Generation) were "wild as goats."

> *In the history of the world, I am aware of no one who was ill served by not drinking at all.*

I have never been a big drinker. The older I get, the less appetite I have for strong drink.

On the other hand, being a Graham from the Glover's Hill Community of Marion County and being a Swafford from Bledsoe County, Tenn., I understand the allure of strong drink.

I am of the opinion that drinking is far more dangerous than marijuana.

I don't mean to brag, but I have been told I can give world class, not to mention, memorable speeches after a few drinks which my college and law school friends remind me about, with unsuppressed delight, of my oratorical brilliance never to be forgotten after a few drinks. I cannot remember any of these inspiring speeches. I am sure they were all exceptional.

I have known great talent wasted as a result of alcohol. I have seen little families destroyed by alcohol with implications that will ripple for generations. Damages will never be repaired caused by alcohol.

Let me give you some advice about drinking:

In the history of the world, I am aware of no one who was ill served by not drinking at all.

If you have children and there have been drinking issues in your family, make sure the kids are made fully aware of the perils of drinking and the fact that drinking to excess is a genetic problem. Scare the kids, if at all possible.

Never drink more than two drinks with a glass of water between the first and second drink. If you can't limit drinking to this amount, you have a problem and you should not be drinking at all.

LIFE'S LESSON:

Follow the above recommendations.

Be fearful about drinking! I have had friends whose lives, careers and families were destroyed beyond repair by alcohol.

Long Funerals and Buying One's Way Into Heaven

By Graham Swafford

$\mathscr{I}$ married Sharon Carson on August 9, 1975, two weeks before I started law school.

Years later, during a family discussion about my marriage to Sharon, my sister opined, "Sharon sure got your posterior in the middle of the road."

At any rate, Sharon was from East Memphis, Tenn.

There are those who think East Memphis, Tenn., might be a little more sophisticated than Marion County, Tenn. I always thought East Memphis sophistication was a little overrated. Millions of people around the world share my views.

> *Apparently, there is a giant difference between country funerals and high-brow East Memphis funerals.*

As I was taking the bar exam, Sharon was packing our worldly possessions preparing to head back to Marion County, Tenn., to begin practicing law with my dad, Sam Bob Raulston and F. Nat Brown.

Sharon took to country living quickly. About the only cultural difference Sharon ever commented on (comparing Memphis to country living) dealt with funerals. Apparently, there is a giant difference between country funerals and high-brow East Memphis funerals (if you know what I mean).

One observation I made fairly early about country funerals, dealt with a situation where the minister did not personally know the deceased. For some reason, country ministers feel compelled (every time) to broadcast whether they knew or did not know the deceased.

Simply stated, in opening remarks, when a country preacher, handling a funeral, proclaims with a tone of apology "that he really did not know the dead guy or gal" then you can expect the funeral to be interminably long and the sermon utterly worthless.

I have learned sophisticated families (defined as folks with a little money or political influence) seem to think, without exception, a big church funeral (which includes a reluctant choir "brow beat" into performing) buttressed by a pretty good preacher (i.e. a feel-good sort of fellow) can preach the deceased into Heaven and thereafter we can all look forward to happily being together in Heaven for all eternity notwithstanding the fact the deceased was a mean-spirited drunken reprobate with a propensity to beat a long string of wives and stole from everybody in town.

LIFE'S LESSON:

Beware of funerals in which a country preacher announces in opening remarks he did not know the deceased. You'll need to get ready for a long, long, long, meaningless service. As you get older, make sure you have used the bathroom before you go to these funerals. It is worse than death sitting through these funeral spectacles when you are about to die to relieve yourself and you are in the middle of the pew.

More important than the above advice, always remember if the deceased did not make peace with the Lord prior to death, a good preacher (nor anyone else for that matter) will not be able to preach the deceased into Heaven regardless of wealth or political influence.

Dangerous Domestic Distractions

By Jimbo Webb
Trenton, Tenn.

*T*he practice of law for the much beloved "country lawyer" can be a rough and tumble profession, especially if you have to survive on the front lines of justice as a "country trial lawyer." It is unfortunately not uncommon these days to hear about litigants or witnesses "going off" on somebody, getting bent out of shape and even fighting.

This is especially true with divorce and child custody cases. For instance, in a recent little country divorce case, my client and I were supposed to spend an entire day inspecting several farms, houses, livestock and a big bunch of tractors. Within nine minutes, we had been dog cussed, hollered at and threatened with a whipping by the unhappy, soon-to-be ex-husband. You may judge me as a coward, but the soon-to-be ex-wife and I decided to swallow our pride and "turn tail and go home."

> *You may judge me as a coward, but the soon-to-be ex-wife and I decided to swallow our pride and 'turn tail and go home.'*

Though this kind of abuse has been going on a long time, I will never forget a very dangerous encounter that happened way back in the early 1980s. I appeared with another fixing-to-be-unwed woman in our gorgeous, three story, Gothic style, circa 1900, courthouse in Trenton, Tenn., for a forensic skirmish in a divorce case. I can remember the judge, who was one of those elderly, wise, southern gentlemen who should have been a tranquil and calming influence on this troubled young couple as well as their respective and respectable counsel. Well, he should have been, but he wasn't. The parties tussled and grappled over houses, cars, kids, child support, attorney's fees, court costs and even what day it was.

You can act calm, professional, poised and reserved all you want, but on the inside, I am pretty sure that most of us attorneys who are still mortal get just a little bit nervous and we start soaking up the contentiousness and acrimony.

Well, this short approximation probably lasted only a few hours, but by the time the divorce trial was over, the former love birds and I, my esteemed opposing counsel, the judge, the clerk, the bailiff and anybody else on the same floor of the courthouse that day were exhausted and not in a happy mood.

The young lady client of mine wasn't too thrilled with the outcome of her divorce case, but she wasn't my most unhappy client ever (which means she wasn't screaming and crying hysterically). Maybe I did obtain a little more justice than my opponent, because I do remember that the husband was *very* unhappy when he left the courtroom that day.

Everyone else in our case left the courtroom going down one set of stairs while I ducked down the other. I was looking forward to getting back to my car, turning on the radio and trying to calm down. I admit that I did have a thought or two as I was making my way down to my car about the "not happy camper" husband that was also leaving the courthouse. I left the building, went down the dozen or so steps and then turned to my right towards where my car was parked ...

BAM!

I was knocked with great force backwards onto the pavement, spread eagle in my J.C. Penney three-piece suit. My imitation leather brief case was lying back over my left shoulder like the subject of a detective's photo at a murder scene. Can you believe it? That low-down-such-and-such had snuck around the courthouse and while I was not looking, sucker punched me with a hay maker punch to my head! As I lay prone on the hard concrete sidewalk, more than slightly addled and disoriented I was trying to decide whether to confront the vicious attacker or try to crawl backwards, get up and run. "Fight or Flight" is a difficult choice during the split second after a smack down, even though all of us red-blooded Alpha male Southern men are always sure, before such an event occurs, that we would always raise up and engage in vigorous and successful self-defense until we subdue our threat. I was raising my head up to take a good look at my assailant and at the same time make this monumental decision ...

I was knocked with great force backwards onto the pavement, spread eagle in my J.C. Penney three-piece suit. My imitation leather brief case was lying back over my left shoulder like the subject of a detective's photo at a murder scene.

This is where Paul Harvey would have promised, after a commercial break, to give us the "rest of the story." In fact, it was a commercial, of sorts, that had actually caused my "assault." You see, what happened was, as I opened those east side doors to the Gibson County Courthouse, I was looking right across the street at a liquor store and in the front window of the liquor store was a full-sized colored poster of a gorgeous young lady in a bikini who was trying to persuade me to come in and buy some rum or tequila or imported beer or such. Well, I was not interested in my "fire water" at that point in the day, but I just thought it was common decency to see all of the "commercial" that the booze company had produced. It seems that when I got to the end of the courthouse steps and then turned right toward my car, my neck had strangely swiveled to maintain my eye target.

I then walked promptly into a parking meter and it was the parking meter that had cold cocked me in the side of the head and caused my fall back to the sidewalk.

When I looked up and realized that my attacker was a stationary metal post and a modified gum ball machine, my thought immediately shifted to other people who could be threatening me, all but in a different way! Witnesses!

Merciful God, there were none.

LIFE'S LESSON:

And now you know ... if you are a country trial lawyer seeking out a living in the world of marital discord: Beware the Dangerous Domestic Distractions!

The Pigs Get Fat and the Hogs Get Slaughtered

By Graham Swafford

*S*everal years ago, I took a real lesson trying a case in federal court. Randy Wilson, an attorney in Chattanooga, Tenn., represented a very large trucking company whom I had sued. The facts were simple. My client, who was pretty fair-looking by the way, was driving down the interstate highway and got "rear-ended" by Randy's client, a speeding-recklessly driven truck owned by a giant, rich, heartless, multi-state trucking company.

What part of the word "giant, rich, multi-state trucking company" do you not understand? What part of the word "rear-ended" do you not understand? Is there any question about "speeding and reckless" that my readers do not understand? Randy's client was just calloused.

How in the world does a lawyer lose a lawsuit like this? I repeat, I had a very likeable client — the BIG truck just slammed into my client from the rear. One would think any lawyer could win this kind of case.

I was full of myself and by this time I had abandoned all common sense.

We tried the case in front of Judge John Y. Powers. I have to admit, my client really wasn't hurt that bad, but she did have some damages and she did have some medical bills and her mother's Lincoln Continental was torn up some.

Randy and I picked the jury pretty quickly. We put on the proof, etc. About midday Judge Powers adjourned court and we all took off for lunch.

I would never brag nor would I want to ever be accused of being overly optimistic but, I thought the case was going pretty well on our end. I knew I had Randy over the barrel. Up until this point, Randy was sort of speechless.

Folks, this lawyer from Marion County was "pouring it on." Things could not have been going better. I was proud of myself.

My client, in addition to being pretty fair looking (not to mention robust if you know what I mean) was a bright gal and she knew things were going well and we had the big trucking company "on the run."

Over lunch, I was mulling over the case with my client and she finally blurts out: "Well, how much are you going to ask for in the closing arguments?"

In reality, I thought the lawsuit was worth about $30-40 thousand, on a good day. I repeat — a real good day. This was not a big lawsuit. I repeat, for those who need additional clarity, this was not the type of lawsuit that I expected to pay for the house. This was not the type of lawsuit which I expected to educate the kids. This was not the type of lawsuit I expected to try and thereafter retire from my law practice. Like I said, this was about a $30-40 thousand lawsuit that any lawyer just could not lose under any circumstances.

At any rate, when the client asked what I was going to ask for in the closing arguments, I told her I would ask for $60-70 thousand and with that she responded: "Oh, this case is going pretty well — let's ask for a lot more than that." To this suggestion I replied without a millisecond of thought: "Sounds good to me."

I point out sometimes monkeys fall out of trees and by this time I was beginning to think this case might be a "monkey."

We proceeded back to the courtroom to finish the trial. Things continued to go well for me. I became more enthused with my representation which is code for "I was full of myself and by this time I had abandoned all common sense."

During a "stem-winding" closing argument, I asked for several hundred thousand dollars. In all modesty, my closing argument was impressive. I was proud of myself. The client was happy.

After I had finished with my closing argument, Randy Wilson stood before the jury and suddenly on a dime the tables turned. Randy Wilson proceeded to hand me my country posterior. Randy pointed out how unreasonable I was. Randy reminded the jury of the word "greed." Randy reminded the jury how I wanted something for nothing. Randy reminded the court that I did not have a bit of proof to demonstrate such an excessive demand. Randy reminded the jury how insincere I was, not to mention it was all a travesty of justice. By the time Randy Wilson got through with his closing argument not only did I look like an unprincipled thief but, admittedly, I was ready to "hide under the table." Heck, my mother and wife would have been rooting for Randy.

Shortly thereafter, the jury received their instructions and went back to deliberate returning very shortly with a verdict. I repeat "very shortly." Very shortly, in the lawsuit business, is code for "the jury had already made up their mind."

With a lawsuit that "couldn't be lost" involving a personable attractive client, with facts representing absolute negligence, with a case involving a calloused trucking company, the jury gave a defense verdict awarding my client "absolutely nothing." It was a stunning loss. I don't know who was more surprised, Randy or me.

For sure the monkey fell out of the tree.

LIFE'S LESSON:
Don't be greedy! Pigs get fat — Hogs get slaughtered!

Stringy Sweet Potatoes

By Anonymous

*I*t was December 1933, depth of the Depression. Anna was a good little girl living in a little town in the South. She had been baptized the year before and was very faithful to church — always present when the doors opened for church, for Sunday school, prayer meetings and BYPU — especially BYPU. That was where they had parties and different projects, which Anna participated in happily. The latest project was collecting food for the poor for Christmas dinner. Anna came home and told Mama about the project. "What can I take, Mama? I have to take something." Mama was in the kitchen making cornbread for dinner. She knew Christmas dinner would be slim at her house but she didn't want to disappoint Anna. "Please, Mama." Finally, Mama said "You can take that bag of sweet potatoes sitting in the corner." The bag was small and the sweet potatoes were stringy looking, but Anna happily took them to BYPU on Sunday.

> *She, herself, had managed to save 29¢ with which to buy presents at the Ten Cent Store.*

Anna no longer really believed in Santa Claus and she knew not to expect much, but she still hoped Mama would be able to get Santa to bring "something" to put in the stocking which she would hang on the back of a chair on Christmas Eve — maybe an orange and an apple or maybe even a real present! She, herself, had managed to save 29¢ with which to buy presents at the Ten Cent Store. You could buy lots of things for 10¢ at the Ten Cent Store. After much thought she had bought a small car for little brother, a five-cent bag of candy for her sister and a handkerchief for daddy. She still didn't know what she could get for Mama with the nine cents she had left, but it was so exciting having something to look forward to: the Christmas pageant where she was one of the angels singing "Glory to God" and of course the party at BYPU. She busied herself decorating the house, making chains of different, colored construction paper and sprigs of holly she picked from the tree in the backyard.

Two days before Christmas, Mrs. Olmstead, wife of one of the deacons, came to the house. She was carrying a package. Mama shyly welcomed her to the kitchen where she opened the package. In it were a doll for little sister, a top for brother, two and a half yards of blue cloth with which mama would later make a new dress for Anna and food! — a chicken, two cans of green beans, a box of cookies and a small bag of stringy, sweet potatoes.

LIFE'S LESSON:

"It is in giving that we receive." You never know what will come around to you again.

What Goes Around Comes Around
(Advice to Young Lawyers)

By Graham Swafford

As you go through life, you will find there are certain laws of nature or rules that are accurate 100 percent of the time without exception. Let me give a couple examples: 2+2=4 or "The sun rises in the east and sets in the west."

With the above certainties in mind, I want to give some advice to young lawyers. This advice is accurate *every time* with scientific or mathematical certainty. Young lawyers can rely upon the following rule with total certainty for the rest of their lives with total predictability.

> *A good, deliberate, indiscriminate backstabbing for no reason happens to all of us at one time or the other including saints and sinners.*

Periodically, one finds himself or herself mistreated, or backstabbed by someone for unknown reasons. Don't be surprised! A good, deliberate, indiscriminate backstabbing for no reason happens to all of us at one time or another including saints and sinners.

Often times, after a particularly good backstabbing, meaningful options are limited. One can bluster and make a bunch of threats (that cannot be backed up) or one can make a fool of oneself, but that's about it.

I can state with absolute certainty "every dog has its day." This quote was intended for the legal profession with 100 percent certainty. It applies to everybody else in the world about 85 percent of the time.

LIFE'S LESSON:

When you are mistreated or stabbed in the back, go home and shut up. Sit tight and wait, but shut up! I repeat — shut up! What goes around comes around! Revenge is best served up cold. Opportunity is always on its way. Forgive in a Biblical sense, but be ready to pull the trigger and remember:
What goes around comes around!

Marital Advice

By Graham Swafford

I am going to give a lesson and/or an observation after which some readers will marvel at my insight and wisdom. Some readers will be infuriated thinking I am sanctimonious and condescending.

No doubt the following life lesson will provide scintillating cocktail conversation for my sophisticated readers.

So here is the background. The facts are always a little different, but always a variation of the same story. I repeat — *always!*

A complete analysis of the topic of compatibility could consume volumes.

A couple times a year Bambi (made up name) comes into the office all dressed up with a look of firm resolve on her face. Bambi is typically defined as a former cheerleader or class favorite (who still looks pretty good for those who pay attention to such), graduated in the top tier of her class, completed college, has a good job, etc., but then married Bubba (made up name) over her family's "strident objections." The term "strident objection" is code for "Bambi's family was mad at Bambi for marrying Bubba and they are still mad."

Bubba is typically defined as a former football player who is down on his luck with a bad back, no job and generally mad at the world, not to mention broke. Simply stated, (if you haven't figured it out by now) Bubba is sort of dumb, no longer cute and funny and has a mean drinking problem all brought about because Bubba is misunderstood. For the uninformed, the term "misunderstood" is code for dumb, lazy and a little crazy.

Typically when Bambi comes into the office she says she wants to know her "options." The word "options" is typically code language for "I have outgrown that dumb, lazy husband of mine and he is driving me crazy — get me out of this marriage!"

In short, Bambi wants to dump Bubba and hit the road.

I point out Bambi is typically still mad (not to mention embarrassed) about having her car repossessed and then being without wheels (for the uninformed, women usually like a nice set of wheels).

For statistical accuracy, my readers might find it interesting that about 30-40 percent of the time Bambi is already scoping her options, if you know what I mean, but usually the new man in the wings is not that big a deal (or at least Bambi doesn't tell me too much about her new love life).

Books, if not entire libraries, have provided scholarly treatment addressing domestic strife, divorce, family breakup, etc.

Let me sum up the "Bambi's" problem (or all domestic relations problems for that matter) in one word. The word is "compatibility."

There are different types of compatibility problems. Particularly when you have a bright girl and a not-so-bright (i.e. dumb) guy, there is always a compatibly problem. Bright girls cannot marry intellectually inferior men — the male becomes intimidated creating deadly problems for the ever present male ego. Not surprisingly, it is not a compatibility problem at all for a bright guy to marry a gal of lesser intelligence (she can be downright dumb for that matter), particularly when the gal has a robust figure. I guess this distinction is just one of the great ironies of life my readers might enjoy pondering.

Money is always a major compatibility issue particularly when the girl comes from a much more prominent family and the guy doesn't make as much money as the girl's dad.

Religion is a compatibility issue which mostly effects future generations.

Alcohol and substance abuse is a compatibility issue, particularly when the male loses his job or gets arrested and Bambi is called in the middle of the night to post bond and get Bubba out of jail.

Family background and heritage can be a compatibility issue.

Never forget sexual compatibility. Some people have a motor always running at fever pitch and some have more modest appetites, if you know what I mean.

A complete analysis of the topic of compatibility could consume volumes.

LIFE'S LESSON:
When giving young lovers marital advice, the first question
to ask is whether the young couple is truly in love or just bored.
Then try to determine if the young couple will be truly com-
patible for the next 50 years.
Compatibility, or lack of compatibility, is typically obvious.

*I expect to get some comments about the above advice. After being married for 39 years and handling hundreds, if not thousands, of divorce cases, my views on this life lesson will not be changed.

Joe Ray Wilson

By Graham Swafford

*Always acknowledge a fault. This will throw those in author-
ity off their guard and give you an opportunity to commit more.*

— *Mark Twain*

One of the most memorable guys I ever met was Joe Ray Wilson.

When I first got out of law school, I arrived back in Marion County, Tenn., and started practicing law. Our major client was the First Bank of Marion County. We represented the First Bank of Marion County from the General Sessions Court all the way to the Supreme Court. In my modest opinion, the First Bank of Marion County consistently received extraordinarily, brilliant, legal advice.

> *"We will never do it again!"*

In reality, the singular reason we represented the First Bank of Marion County is that Joe Ray Wilson and my father were best friends. Joe Ray and my dad knew each other for decades. They went off to war together and they were partners in business deals, etc. Looking back at it, I do not believe competent, legal counsel had a thing in the world to do with our representation of the First Bank of Marion County.

While not meaning to shock Mick or Jane (Joe Ray and Juanita's kids) my guess is that my father and Joe Ray Wilson "will carry secrets to the grave." I admire the fidelity of friendship my father and Joe Ray enjoyed.

Joe Ray had certain unmatched talents for running a business, particularly a bank. While running the First Bank of Marion County, Joe Ray could "make a decision on a dime" and never look back. Joe Ray might have been in error at times, but he was "never in doubt," nor did he enjoy being second guessed for that matter.

I learned a great lesson from Joe Ray that I use *every day of the week.*

The First Bank of Marion County was an everyday client. The fine folks at the First Bank of Marion County were always up to something — something was always "cooking," if you know what I mean. They always needed a lawyer for something, for which I was happy to accommodate.

Periodically, not to mention on a *regular* basis, I would get wind of some danger or pending peril at the First Bank.

I would promptly dispatch myself to the First Bank of Marion County to single handedly save the day not to mention the First Bank's unsuspecting investors from total calamity.

I would walk into Joe Ray's office and immediately attack the problem. Joe Ray would listen attentively and every time would then say "Golly, I did not know we were doing wrong. I did not know it would make you mad." Joe Ray would immediately apologize and say "we will never do it again." Joe Ray would thank me for coming down and express appreciation for our stewardship and once again summarize with "We will never do it again."

After about the third or fourth "I'm sorry, we will never do it again" I would typically be totally disarmed, at which time we would all start laughing. I would then tell Joe Ray, John Moore, Raymond Vinson and the staff what a fine job they were doing. You would think I was congratulating the Federal Reserve.

I would then drive back to the office feeling a bit embarrassed that I had even gone down to the bank to express my concern to such financial titans as Joe Ray and the staff at the First Bank. Needless to say, I would typically be so befuddled I would not send Joe Ray a bill — a policy he approved without exception.

Usually about a week later it would dawn on me that Joe Ray had just "worked me again." It happened every time.

LIFE'S LESSON:

Learned from Joe Ray Wilson: When you mess up big time, admit your mistake quickly and smile. Apologize quickly and smile. Repeat at least three times "Golly, I'll never do that again" and smile. Thank your critic for showing concern and smile. Then at least three more times profusely thank your critic for their concern, support and friendship and smile. Then say once again and in closing "I will never do it again!" and smile.

Trust me the above lesson works "every time."

If Martha Stewart had consulted with Joe Ray, not only would she not have gone to jail, but she would have saved billions and been applauded as a business leader for candor, courage and integrity.

If Bruce Pearl had learned the Joe Ray trick not only would he be the University of Tennessee's men's basketball coach but he would probably be athletic director at the University and the University of Tennessee would name a street after him. Pearl would have then written inspirational books applauding integrity.

If Richard Nixon had consulted Joe Ray, I believe without

a doubt the controversy which ended his presidency would have blown over in three weeks and Watergate would not be in our vocabulary. I don't believe over one million people would have been killed at the calamitous conclusion of the Vietnam war.

Bill Clinton would have saved himself untold grief and embarrassment if he had consulted with Joe Ray.

The list of those who could have benefited from the lesson of "Joe Ray" is simply endless.

*Note: Joe Ray passed peacefully October 7, 2011. I think of Joe Ray every day — what an education. I assure you I passed the Joe Ray lesson to my children.

Sex Advice

By Graham Swafford

*Q*uestion: What are two things King David, Bill Clinton, Rev. Ted Haggard, Rev. Jimmy Swaggart, Liz Taylor, Rev. Jim Baker, LeAnn Rimes, Tiger Woods, Arnold Schwarzenegger, John Edwards, David Letterman, former Congressman Anthony Weiner, General David Patraeus (former director of the CIA) along with millions and millions of other people throughout the history of the world all have in common?

I repeat — *all* have in common?

Answer: The first thing they all have in common is they got caught running around. The second thing they all have in common is not withstanding their superior intelligence and talent, not one of them thought they would get caught.

Having shed light on the above question, I point out no respectable, self-improvement and/or inspirational book about small town life would be complete without SEX.

Sex sells and I want to sell some of these books — the proceeds go for a good cause.

To make my book more marketable, I want to mention in graphic detail, for my readers enjoyment, toe curling, screaming, heels to the ceiling, sweating, howling, heavy breathing, panting sex.

I want my readers' imagination to get as wild as their mind will allow. Folks, remember the South Pittsburg boat dock and Coppinger Cove (not to mention other little "hot spots" if you catch my drift).

I remember one case in particular where we obtained an annulment for a young lady, which in the opinion of her father, included the restoration of her virginity. Let any law firm in America top that for results.

Tell all your friends my book includes "lurid sex" (not to mention familiar names), which will ensure thousands of copies are sold.

But first I would like to point out, with complete modesty, that at the Swafford, Jenkins and Raines Law Firm all of our clients conduct themselves, at all times, with sobriety and propriety. *All* of our clients are chaste, if not downright virginal, and have always been so.

On the other hand, our law firm has acquired some knowledge (not to mention experience) about personal indiscretions from the ever-present gossip mill.

Not to boast (or try to drum up business with the promises of spectacular legal results) but I remember one case in particular where we obtained an annulment for a young lady, which in the opinion of her father, included the restoration of her virginity. Let any law firm in America top that for results. I suppose our results were debatable. Everybody left happy. The young lady left with a smile on her face — if you know what I mean. The young lady still grins when we meet.

'Do you think she can keep a secret?'

Since the beginning of time, sex has always been a topic that seems to fascinate people, cause wars, creates scintillating (not to mention entertaining) conversation/gossip, etc.

In particular, "running around on your spouse sex" seems to hold limitless fascination, not to mention produces shocked gasps of disbelief from both small town prudes and big city sophisticates who have not been caught. I point out, lawyers since the beginning of time have benefited from endless litigation involving this type shenanigans.

I remember on one occasion a member of respectable proper society (usually defined as someone who has some money or political connections) was regretfully explaining a momentary indiscretion and uttered a profound observation:

"If it flies, if it floats, if it is a limited partnership, or it will get intimate, just rent it, but don't buy it."

This statement was memorable, and you would not believe *who* gave me this pearl of wisdom.

Another sage member of upper crust proper society (who over a period of time had made a fortune he did not want to lose in a messy divorce) made the following "running around" recommendation which I suppose carries some wisdom:

"If you're going to run around, make sure it is at least a hundred miles away from Marion County and make sure her husband makes more money than you do."

I thought this was good advice. Once again, my readers would howl with delight if they knew who shared this bit of wisdom with me.

On a more practical note, another circumspect scholar stated when he was contemplating an impropriety, "do you think she can keep a secret?"

Last, but not least, another well-known, but fallen saint who had acquired an agricultural background before he made a serious fortune, sadly mused in my office:

"Don't ride the working stock — Don't work the riding stock."

All the above represent not only great advice but makes for entertaining conversation, not to mention useful quotes.

Here is the point: Sooner, if not later, you will get caught — every time — no matter how brilliant you are. Don't fool yourself!

LIFE'S LESSON:

If you're going to run around, you will get caught. Your spouse will be less than pleased. Everybody in town will talk about it with expressions of fake (and I repeat — fake) shock and disbelief. Most will gloat, not to mention enjoy your misery.

If you have accumulated any money, running around on a spouse could potentially cost you a fortune.

More tragic than any of the above, your children will pay an incalculable price which has the potential of going places you do not dream.

Those inclined to ignore the above advice will ultimately recognize my great wisdom.

---

*Note: I did not make this story or these quotes up — about all I can say is "welcome to the practice of law!"

Mother's Love

By Senator Roy Herron
Dresden, Tenn.

$\mathcal{M}$other was born in 1916 in the "Sweet Potato Capital of the World," Gleason, Tenn. A few weeks later her parents moved eight miles to Dresden, the county seat of Weakley County. They moved to a house two blocks from the court square and two blocks from the city limits. On that same small lot, Mother has lived seven of her eight decades and lives there still.

When Mother was a tiny baby, John Irvine, the proprietor of Irvine's Grocery, would call my grandmother on sunshiny days and tell her, "Johnnie, get the baby ready; I'm going to take her around today and show her off."

Mr. Irvine would bring Miss Johnnie's groceries and empty the wire basket on her kitchen table. Then they would fill the basket with a pillow and lay Mother on it, and cover her with a baby blanket. Mr. Irvine would leave with Mother swinging in the basket on his arm. He would place her carefully next to him on the seat, then slowly drive his horse and wagon around town. Each time he stopped, he would carry the basket with Mother in one hand and a basket of groceries in the other. They would go to the back door, where the delighted customer always insisted they come in so she could see the new baby, Mary Cornelia Brasfield.

Maybe the grocer was just shrewd at marketing. But as Mother grew up hearing the story of Mr. Irvine taking her around, she always felt special. And she was.

When we were growing up, Mother repeatedly told my younger brother Ben and me about distinguished ancestors. She said our people fought for the Colonies in the Revolutionary War.

She claimed that in the Battle of King's Mountain no less than 10 relatives, a father and nine sons were killed.

But her favorite story was about an ancestor named Reuben Edmonston.

"Now, your several-greats-grandfather, Reuben Edmonston, was the first settler here in Weakley County," Mother would brag. "He and his brother-in-law John Bradshaw came here in 1819, when no one else was around except for the Chickasaw Indians, who didn't really stay here. They built the first log cabin in the county and raised the first patch of corn. They settled on Mud Creek, about six miles from here towards Martin — but of course there was no Dresden or Martin back then. There wasn't even a Weakley County until four years later."

"You've heard about Davy Crockett," Mother would say, knowing we'd seen the movie and devotedly watched the television show. "People think Davy Crockett was such a great frontiersman, but he followed your ancestor Reuben Edmonston to West Tennessee. Davy Crockett owned land in this county, too, not far from our farm at the Forks of the River, after Reuben Edmonston settled here."

"You know that Davy Crockett was the champion bear hunter. But do you know who was second? Your ancestor Reuben Edmonston. One year Davy killed over 100 bears, but Reuben got almost as many, 80-something, I think."

I wondered why she told these old tales of ancient ancestors, until I finally realized she wished she'd been a pioneer.

To understand Mother, and why she'd have liked being a pioneer, you have to understand her parents.

Mother's father, Roy Brasfield, became a pharmacist in 1913. Some said the center of activity in Dresden was the Alexander and Brasfield drug store. If so, the epicenter was the drug store's soda fountain. Mother was allowed all of the ice cream, sundaes and milk shakes she wanted, though fountain drinks and candy were forbidden.

I wondered why she told these old tales of ancient ancestors, until I finally realized she wished she'd been a pioneer.

Mr. Roy soon proved himself a popular friend and a successful businessman. He needed to succeed, because many customers could pay little or nothing. He filled their prescriptions just the same, as long as they tried to pay something, or if they were unable to work. He also needed to make a profit, because his wife, Miss Johnnie, was becoming the town's unpaid social worker.

When Miss Johnnie moved to Dresden, she had immediately joined the First Methodist Episcopal Church. She thought the church doors could not open without her entering: Sunday mornings, Sunday evenings, Wednesday Bible studies. Her Missionary Society met on Mondays — and their work continued through the week. It seemed to Mother that if the sun came up, Miss Johnnie went down to the church.

Miss Johnnie took Mister Jesus mighty seriously. She read and re-read those troubling words about The Great Judgment. She could quote the 25th chapter of Matthew from memory and often did, teaching her daughter and reminding her neighbors:

> *"And before him shall be gathered all nations; and he shall separate them one from another, as a shepherd divideth his sheep from the goats;*
>
> *And he shall set the sheep on his right hand, but the goats on the left. Then shall the King say unto them on his right hand, Come, ye*

blessed of my Father, inherit the kingdom prepared for you from the foundation of the world:

For I was a hungred, and ye gave me meat; I was thirsty, and ye gave me drink; I was a stranger, and ye took me in;

Naked and ye clothed me; I was sick, and ye visited me; I was in prison, and ye came unto me.

Then shall the righteous answer him, saying, Lord, when saw we thee a hungred, and fed thee? Or thirsty, and gave thee drink?

When saw we thee a Stanger, and took thee in? Or naked, and clothed thee?

Or when saw we thee sick, or in prison, and came unto thee?

And the King shall answer and say unto them, Verily I say unto you, Inasmuch as ye have done it unto one of the least of these my brethren, ye shall have done it unto me." (King James Version)

When Miss Johnnie died in 1952, a Memphis newspaper reported, "She was what the town said was an 'angel of mercy', visiting in homes in Dresden whenever there was sorrow or distress, bearing messages of cheer and good will."

> ***Miss Johnnie took Mister Jesus mighty seriously.***

But Miss Johnnie went bearing more than messages. Barely five feet tall, her tiny legs carried her rapidly all over town, taking whatever the sick needed and the poor could not afford. Baskets of groceries for the hungry. Home-cooked meals for the sick. Clean sheets for poor women to lie on as they gave birth. Medicines from her husband's drug store, knowing that many could never pay and none were ever billed. When the Mississippi River flooded, she spent weeks at the church, cooking and caring for the refugees, many of them poor sharecroppers. When the Depression hit, she just did even more of the same.

She did what she did, like many church women and some men, because Jesus told her to and she took Jesus seriously. She knew what Jesus taught because she herself taught "the littlest children." Miss Johnnie went out and gathered children, convincing parents to let their children come, even when poverty made parents reluctant to attend the Methodist Church where the more affluent went. And for more than 30 years she gathered the children around her "horseshoe table" and showed how Jesus loved them.

Miss Johnnie has been dead a half-century, yet people still tell me, "Your grandmother taught me in Sunday School. She loved us so, and I loved her!"

Miss Johnnie died the year before I was born. Those who knew her and know my Mother tell me I didn't miss a thing. They have seen her faithful compassion and love live on in my Mother.

Mother's father, Mr. Roy, was less angelic. At times he was even a bit devilish, inviting preachers for a quiet drink in his kitchen, much to his tee-totaling wife's chagrin. But he still gave medicines and supplies to those he knew could never pay. And he paid the bills for the sheets and groceries his wife gave the poor and sick.

While Mr. Roy sometimes complained about his wife's unconventional ways, he encouraged his daughter to do whatever she could do. He was determined not to let her gender or others' sexism stop or even slow his darling girl who was never still, always getting into things, always having too much to do. By the time Mother was five, a neighbor had nicknamed her "Friskie," and that suited Mr. Roy (and Mother) just fine.

He taught Mother to swim so early that she never remembered when she couldn't. She swam as well or better than the boys, which created its own problems.

When Mother was nine years old, her Sunday School Class went to Fulton, Kentucky to a real swimming pool (instead of a river or a pond). Mother played with the girls at what she considered "the baby end" of the pool, but then decided she would swim with the boys in the deep end. Her Sunday school teacher, Dr. Jones, didn't like it and told Mother so. She stubbornly went ahead playing with the boys in the deep end, having a good time.

Mother was sick the next Sunday so she missed Sunday school, but a cousin went and heard Dr. Jones tell about the girl who swam with the boys and how that was "unladylike and unChristian." The next morning a still-furious Mr. Roy marched off to see Dr. Jones and told him he had no right to try to keep Mother "down there with the sissy girls." Furthermore, he made it clear he did not appreciate Dr. Jones talking about his beloved daughter.

That wasn't the last time Mother refused to stay in her place and enjoyed her father's support.

When Mother wanted to roller skate with older kids to another town, she knew better than to ask her mother. She went to Mr. Roy who pointed out that the journey would be almost 20 miles. "I know," Mother impatiently replied. "But, please, can I, please, Daddy?" Mr. Roy hesitated, then smiled and replied, "If you think you can do it, you can." And she did.

Soon stories came back to the drug store of his daughter's escapades on skates. Near his store was a hill with a sidewalk and several concrete steps. Mr. Roy was amused when customers would tell him that "your daredevil daughter" was skating down the sidewalk, jumping the steps, and landing on the sidewalk below. He was proud when he learned that only two children in town, the other an older boy, would even attempt the leap.

One year when the fair came to town, so did a barn-storming airplane that took passengers up for short rides. When Miss Johnnie heard about it, she strictly prohibited Mother from getting in that plane.

So Mother went to the drug store and begged her father to take her in the plane. He responded, "You know your Mother would not be amused if she found out we did such."

"Then, Daddy," Mother smiled, "we simply mustn't tell her."

That wasn't the last time Mother refused to stay in her place.

Soon they were at the Fairgrounds, in a crowd where everyone knew everyone, waiting their turn to ride.

Mother sat in Mr. Roy's lap in the backseat of the two-seater open-cockpit biplane and they took to the air. Mr. Roy wasted no time in directing the pilot toward the court square so they could wave to the crowd. Then Mr. Roy could not resist. He had the pilot fly over the little house on the corner of Cedar and Main, and then repeatedly buzz their home — and Miss Johnnie.

Mother's parents wanted her to avoid the fate of most young women at that time: no education beyond high school and an early marriage. They told her of their plans to send her to a fine women's college. But Mother, always strong-willed, made other plans. She had met a young man from Greenfield, 12 miles away. He was four years older, perhaps too much older, but handsome, well-mannered, and from a good family. And she fell hard for him.

Forty years later I was a high school senior when I asked Mother to go with me to help start the car whose battery had died the night before on a country road. She asked if I had been alone, knowing that I had not been. As I drove us closer to the car, Mother started grinning. By the time we got within a half mile of the town's teenage parking spot, Mother started chuckling. As we pulled around a corner and the car came into view, Mother laughed out loud. My 17-year-old pride already plenty wounded, I told her it was not funny.

"Oh, yes, it is," she quickly replied. "This is exactly where your father and I went 40 years ago."

"Everyone," Mother recalls, "was going out of state to marry. It seemed the thing to do. Very few had any money for big weddings." Nine days after she turned 18, on October 28, 1934, Mother and Dad went to Wickliffe, Ky., and were married by a Methodist minister in the home of a justice of the peace.

Each returned to their parents' homes that evening and kept the secret of their wedding. Mother continued her senior year of high school. She hid her wedding ring above the transom in her bedroom, sneaking it out in her shoe to wear when she and Dad went on dates.

In December, Dad fell very ill. His mother grew so worried that she told him if he would just get well, she'd do anything for him. Why, he could even marry that little girl over in Dresden. Dad opened his eyes and said, "I already did."

She hid her wedding ring above the transom in her bedroom, sneaking it out in her shoe to wear when she and Dad went on dates.

His shocked mother fled the room and found her husband, telling him the awful news. Clarence, however, liked Mother and was pleased. He called the drug store and told Mr. Roy the news. He suggested, "I guess this married couple ought to live together. If it's acceptable to you, Mr. Brasfield, I'll be over later this afternoon to pick Mary up."

Mr. Roy was disappointed and angry that his teenager had eloped. His and Miss Johnnie's plans for college the next year were suddenly moot. He left the drug store and walked the couple of blocks to the school. He got Mother out of class and told her, "You've played the Devil, young lady, but I'll stick with you."

Miss Johnnie was deeply hurt because her daughter did not have a church wedding. And because Miss Johnnie had dreamed for her daughter a very different life.

Mother and Dad lived with his parents and she commuted from Greenfield to finish high school. In a couple of years, they had my older brother, followed four years later by my sister. Then came the war.

Mother survived the war and Dad's absence with the help of her parents and friends. Then Dad came home. But for Mother, unbelievably, life got harder. When I think of Mother and the strength of her character, I think of what happened right after the war. None of her pioneer ancestors had more courage, or were more heroic, than she was when at one point her husband, her two children and even the baby she carried inside her all were struggling to survive.

Dad had entered a Memphis hospital again, with still more complications from his war wounds. He was fighting infections and struggling to survive. The doctors were recommending amputating at least one leg. At the same time, my sister was at home with measles, threatened by fevers of 104 and 105. Back then measles was a killer and Betsye was in grave danger. Meanwhile, my brother Dean, like his Dad, was in a hospital, the one at Paris. He was seriously ill with pneumonia. At that time, many died of pneumonia; Mother feared her firstborn would be another.

Mother was running from the hospital in Memphis to their home to the hospital in Paris, back and forth, trying to take care of everyone all at once. One day as she hurried out of the hospital to go see Betsye, she fell down the stairs and miscarried.

How did she deal with everything, when the lives of her husband and two children were threatened and the life within her was lost? Amazingly, that may not have been the worst time, because there also were rough times later, after I was born.

> *'He never was drunk, he thought, when he was that a way. He couldn't stand up many a time and he wasn't drunk.'*

When my younger brother Ben and I were growing up, Dad had sober days and lots of them. In fact, almost all the days we shared with him he was sober. His nights, however, sometimes were different. He would come in from work and go to the cabinet where the bottles were. Sometimes he drank but a little. Other times, he drank too much. I can still see Mother trying to maneuver him back to the bedroom, trying to keep him from going out and driving off.

I once asked Mother about the toughest thing she ever encountered. She replied without hesitation: "Your Daddy's drinking. That was the only time he wasn't in pain. And I understood. But I hated the drinking with a passion. He was a good man, just—ooohh," and she shuddered. "I blamed myself for a long time. What have I done? What could I do? From the second drink on, he was ... from the fourth one he was mean ... He never hit me but one time. And then he choked me one time."

"He followed me from the kitchen to the bedroom. He pushed me against the chest of drawers and grabbed me by the throat. There were marks on my throat. I wore something high collared for a few days. You were seven or eight at the time. You tried to come in there and he told you to get away from the door. You knew something was wrong."

"He never was drunk, he thought, when he was that a way. He couldn't stand up many a time and he wasn't drunk."

I do not condemn my Father for what professionals call "self-medicating." In fact, I am in awe that he endured the pain he did, as well as he did, for as long as he did. I could not have endured his pain for three days, much less three decades. But I am at least as amazed that Mother was strong enough to endure both the pain Dad suffered and also the pain he inflicted.

Then, when she was 50, she almost had to bury him.

On the late afternoon of October 5, 1967, I came home to find neighbors in the house and my father on the floor. Mother had sent my brother Ben to get Lloyd Reavis Jr. who lived two doors away and when Mr. Reavis came he called the funeral home for the ambulance. "Dead Man" Joe Anderson (to distinguish from the optometrist named Joe Anderson) rushed over. They loaded Dad on the stretcher, got him in the ambulance and Mother jumped in the back with him.

They drove to Union City on the two-lane road at 90 and 100 miles an hour. Dad regained consciousness long enough to tell Joe not to kill him with his driving. But Joe didn't slow down, passing cars and running others off the road. In Union City, the doctor and nurses were outside waiting. Then it was Mother's turn to wait.

When the doctor finally came back out, he told Mother she ought to kiss that ambulance driver. If he had been 10 minutes later getting to the hospital, Dad would have been dead.

I grew up in the same house that Mother did, the same house where she still lives. Within two blocks of Mother's home in her lifetime have lived the governor, a state public service commissioner, at least five mayors, five state legislators, four or five judges, a county judge and a county executive, other courthouse officials, and countless members of the county court, the county commission, and the city council.

We were two houses down and across the street from Aunt Carrie Pentecost, who long was the center of politics in Weakley County and some would maintain in Tennessee. As her son once observed of our neighborhood, referring to his own mother's home: "Tom Seaver could stand in her front yard and throw a baseball not more than twice, maybe just once, and hit where every one of these elected officials lived."

When Aunt Carrie's kinfolks came to visit, they included our mutual neighbor and her great-nephew, Gov. Ned McWherter, her niece and nephew, Pauline Gore who was one of the first women to graduate from Vanderbilt Law School and Pauline's husband U.S. Senator Albert Gore Sr., and her great-nephew, then U.S. Senator and later Vice President Al Gore.

But the neighborhood was filled not only with "the e-lite and the po-lite" of politics. In every house were those who might not be blood kin but who watched over Mother and then my siblings and me as aunts and uncles, additional mothers and fathers. They watched over us as if we were their own. And we knew they were watching over and after us. Maybe that's why Mother only left briefly and always came back to the same spot of ground. Because she knew how she had been watched over and loved and she wanted nothing less for her own children.

Mother's uniquely Southern double name, Mary Cornelia, is pronounced "Ma-ree Ca Nee-eel-ya." My cousins from North Carolina thought for years that her name was American Eagle.

A college friend came and spent a weekend with us. Lane went back to the city and, referring to my Mother and a character on The Andy Griffith Show and Mayberry RFD, declared, "I just met the real Aunt Bee."

Another visitor, who later became my bride, had to learn not to compliment Mother's antiques and decorations, because every time she did Mother would try to give the items to her.

> *Mother is the epitome of the best of her generation of Southern womanhood — a genuine confluence of Southern respectability and a deeply generous heart.*

My wife says Mother is the epitome of the best of her generation of Southern womanhood — a genuine confluence of Southern respectability and a deeply generous heart. She frets over any negative remarks "being told around town" while preening over positive comments, especially concerning her children or grandchildren.

She was in her seventies and it was the 1990s before she would go to the drug store without first having her hair done and without stockings, pumps and a matching purse.

Mother always has insisted, like her own mother did, that every question from an elder be answered with "Yes, Ma'am" or "No, Ma'am" or "Yes, Sir" or "No, Sir." For Mother, this is not some empty gesture or dead litany, but a sign of deep respect for the hearer — and respectability for the speaker. Recently a dear friend of Mother's died. They had known each other for eight decades and had helped each other through many crises, including their husbands dying within a week of each other. The friend was slightly older than Mother, so until the day she died Mother would not call her by her first name, instead referring to her as Mrs. Riggs.

Despite her deep concern that she and her family be respected and respectable, her door was always open to anyone in need, regardless of social status. Mother simply is the most accepting, embracing, warmest person I ever knew. She learned the values from her mother, her father, and the neighbors and friends who loved them and her.

One family was infamous as the area's poorest, as well as most prolific. At any mention of the family, we kids made faces and made fun. Of course, it was this family's children Mother took home to bathe, de-lice, inspect all over, put in new clothes, brag on and love on. When she returned them to our elementary school, she kissed the children. The little girl hugged Mother's neck and would not let go. Mother's actions created a stir among some of my friends and hers, too, but she went right ahead.

Nor did she stop when she created an even bigger stir by giving family funeral plots to a couple with lots of illness, not much life expectancy, and no money. Mother soon heard that some friends with plots nearby were upset. It wasn't fit for "those people" to be buried there, and what was Mary Cornelia thinking?

"I don't know why they care," Mother sadly told my wife. "They'll be dead then and it won't matter who they're next to."

Many times I would come in from school to find some struggling soul at our kitchen table. "I was just going," the person often would explain. "Just wanted to see your Mama a bit."

Those at the kitchen table included a neighbor who never seemed quite right, some great pain having bent her so. There were women whose children or grandchildren were struggling or ill. Sometimes children came needing a kind adult to care. Sometimes it was their mothers, struggling with husbands or without them. Those that others refused to listen to, Mother invited in and made feel at home. "We all need friends," she would say.

Mornings were Mother's time of day. I suppose I would think that, since when I was a baby she and Dad used to wake me up at three and four o'clock in the morning to play with me. When later I demanded to know why they had done such a silly thing, Mother sheepishly replied that they had not had a baby around in a long time.

When I was a little older, I returned the favor by coming back into their bed in the wee hours of the morning. She would let me snuggle between her and Dad. Many mornings Dad would get up to get coffee for both of them and bring it back to the bedroom. Mother would get up and sit on the side of the bed, rubbing Dad's painful legs. They would drink their coffee and talk and enjoy that time together. I would pretend to be asleep. They would pretend to think I was asleep, and then say those things they wanted me to hear. "Aren't we proud of him?" "Isn't he just the finest boy?"

Christmas is Mother's time of year. She never shines more brightly than at Christmas. None of the children or grandchildren gets more excited than Mother.

The whole house has to be decorated for Christmas. Every room has to have the special touches. Mother goes around the house, putting on her father's old wooden duck decoys little red construction paper hats with white cotton ball trim. The big old candle, started six decades ago by dripping smaller candles onto a wine bottle, has to be placed by the door, so guests can stop and drip more candles on it. The tree ought to be a live cedar from our farm, hung with multicolored lights that somehow even while sitting quietly in boxes in the attic become impossibly tangled and have to be wrestled with before they can be strung again.

When brother Ben and I started duck hunting together on Christmas, Mother still insisted we all open our gifts when we first got up. "It wouldn't be Christmas morning if we didn't open gifts," she explained. So, to leave the house by four o'clock, Mother and Dad and Ben and I would get up at two-thirty or three. While we males staggered sleepily around, Mother bounced like the Labrador puppy we used to hunt with, pointing and loving on us almost more than we could stand at that hour.

Mother has always loved to go. It didn't matter where, she was ready.

Mother grew up between two of the finest fishing lakes in the South. To the east was Kentucky Lake, created by a Tennessee Valley Authority dam. To the west was Reelfoot Lake, created by the earthquakes of 1811 and 1812. Before I was born, Mom developed into a first-class fisherwoman. She would take loads of boys to Kentucky Lake who helped her fill 10-gallon milk cans with crappie.

Then Dad bought a trailer and put it at Reelfoot Lake where we came to know a gentleman named Elbert Spicer. He was a legend. He'd called and hunted ducks with the very best of the very best. For decades. Until when he was in his seventies he decided he was going to die. Then he went to bed to die. After several months passed, he decided maybe he was not going to die, at least not yet. So, he got out of the bed and took up where he had left off: drinking whiskey, chasing young women too young to be his granddaughters, hunting ducks, and fishing.

"Mr. Elbert" knew where the fish were and how to catch them. One day he said to Mother, "Mrs. Judge, the crappie are getting 'bout right. If you'd like to go, I'd be proud to take you."

Mother thought about it and instantly knew two things. First, he was not trying to get her alone, since she was but 30 years his junior and thus far too old to interest him. Secondly, she knew he could catch fish. Soon they took off for one of Mr. Elbert's favorite spots. He took a cane pole, placed the minnows on Mom's double hooks, and before he could get his own pole baited, Mom was catching fish.

When Mom would swing the pole up and the line and fish over the boat, Mr. Elbert would grab the crappie and take it off the hook, rebait Mom's hook, and put her in business again. Then he'd paddle the boat back where he wanted it, but before he could get his own line in the water again, Mom would have another fish — or two. Finally Mr. Elbert could stand it no longer: "Mrs. Judge," he begged, "do you reckon you'd mind if l fished a little, too?"

"Well, of course not, Mr. Spicer," Mom replied. "I've been baiting my own hooks and taking my own fish off for 40 years and I don't mind a bit."

Soon they both were pulling in fish as fast as they could and competing to see who could catch the most.

After that Mr. Elbert always thought Mrs. Judge was special.

Mother has always loved to go. It didn't matter where, she was ready. That was good, because Dad often would come home and say, "Let's go" and we would.

When my younger brother Ben and I were in high school, our parents went to Europe. While they were gone, Ben started riding Brahma bulls and bareback broncs — he is, after all, Mother's son. When they got home and learned of Ben's new hobby, Dad was delighted, his own father having been a cowboy out West for a time. Mother, however, was not amused. In fact, she was terrified that her baby was climbing on huge Brahma bulls.

After that, Mother would not take a long trip without us. Finally, when Ben and I were in college, they went away for 10 days, including one weekend. That weekend, Ben planned to start sky-diving. Unfortunately, his first jumps got rained out. And even Ben would not try it with Mom and Dad back home. Ben really is Mother's son and the far bravest child. His idea of a weekend now is kayaking the roughest water in the Eastern U.S. or going for still wilder streams in Colorado.

In 1976, Dad and Mom bought a new pickup and went to Alaska. By the next spring, he was gone. We children all thought that when Dad died, Mother might not be far behind. Instead, she began the mourning that continues to this day, then she went on living.

She went to Hawaii. She also took her first cruise. In her late sixties, she started riding buses to visit her children and grandchildren.

In her seventies, she first rafted white water. And she started fishing again. In her 78th year, my brother Dean took her fishing at his home on Timms Ford Lake. At my brother's boat dock, he fixed Mom up with a cane pole, but Mother could not see the bobber. For over 20 years Mother has been losing her sight to macular degeneration. She has some peripheral vision, but essentially now only can see light and dark. So, she got down on her hands and knees on the dock, put her face so close to the water her head almost touched the bobber, and held the fishing line in her hands.

Soon she had a bite and with a squeal she yanked the line and pulled out a big brim. Immediately after Dean pulled the fish off her hook and helped her rebait, she was back on her hands and knees, face close to the bobber. In a few minutes she caught a half dozen brim, as happy as if she'd caught Moby Dick.

Even as she has gone blind, she has continued to live at home and alone, fiercely independent, strong even in weakness and perhaps especially in adversity, tough as any. A few days after the family gathered for Mother's 80th birthday party, she went to the doctor. Not eagerly, not even willingly, but only after my wife Nancy learned Mother had fallen in the yard and had to be helped back in the house. When the reluctant patient heard the cardiologist say on Wednesday that a pacemaker might restore her energy and strength, she was ready to have the surgery that day. She grudgingly consented to wait until Monday.

In discussing the procedure with Mother, Dr. Hall explained that the pacemaker's battery lasted eight years and then had to be replaced. My 80-year-old Mother's only question: "Can you do that replacement here also?"

As good a Mother as she is, in another role she excels even more, or so say six grandsons and two great-granddaughters. Not long ago, Mother was dreading going back into the hospital again. She did not want to go, but knew the doctors were right that something was wrong. She got her courage up once again, this time this way, telling Nancy and me: "Your little boys are my reason for living. I want to stick around long enough for them to remember me."

Loving children, all God's children, has been her reason for living for a long time.

Recently Mother flew in a small plane, the first time since her father and the barnstormer took her aloft 70 years earlier.

I marvel that a woman who lives in the same house where she grew up and frequently sleeps on the same bed where she gave birth to her firstborn is always so eager to go. In recent years, sometimes her sense of adventure has been dampened a bit by her sense of propriety. It embarrasses her to go out to eat because she cannot see the food on her plate and is horrified she might spill something. Still, she frequently screws up her courage, tugs on her girdle, and takes off on a new adventure.

Last year, the year she turned 82, I asked what she would like for a Mother's Day gift. So, for the first time in the more than two decades since Dad died, she fished at Reelfoot Lake, this time with all her children and her youngest grandsons.

Knowing how much she enjoyed that fishing trip and thinking we might do something similar, the other day I asked Mother what fun things she'd like to do that she had not yet done.

My 82-year-old mother replied that she would like to go up in a hot air balloon, pilot a plane, and go to the moon.

LIFE'S LESSON:

The epitome of the best of Southern womanhood: A genuine confluence of Southern respectability and a deeply generous heart. This, combined with a daredevil sense of adventure and a strong love for all of God's children, make for a very special person.

Cigarettes, Lying and Proper Society

By Graham Swafford

Times have changed. In recent years, medical and health journals worldwide have been flooded with information concerning the fact that cigarettes and tobacco are bad for you.

When I was a lad growing up in South Pittsburg, Tenn., advertisements flooded the media with tobacco promotions. I still remember one tobacco advertisement boldly announced that "Chesterfield Cigarettes" was the choice of medical doctors.

All the doctors I knew smoked like chimneys.

Apparently, the dangers of tobacco has only recently been medically discovered and documented. I would like to announce my mother, Claude Swafford of Marion County, Tenn., was the first person in the entire world to discover the medical/health risks of cigarettes, not to mention she also pointed out smoking was a garden-variety sin. As we all know, sin is wrong and my mother opposed sin.

> *...we felt we were worldly and wise, not to mention cigarettes seemed to stimulate good conversation. Chris and I were good conversationalists.*

In the face of my mother's warnings concerning the dangers, not to mention the sin of cigarettes, one can but imagine my response. I could not wait to smoke a cigarette! I repeat — I could not wait!

Fortunately or unfortunately (however you look at it), opportunity to sin was just over the horizon. The Hammonds (another unforgettable, not to mention impressive, family) lived directly across from us. My best friend, Chris Hammond (who later went on to play center on the University of Georgia football team), was able to acquire (steal to be more specific) some cigarettes from his parents.

When Chris would steal cigarettes we would quickly sneak off to the woods to happily smoke our ill-acquired treasure, have a little fun and generally sin. Fifty years later, I still thrill with the remembrance of the experience of being a young sinner. My readers would have enjoyed being with Chris and me — smoking and sin was just plain fun! I wish I could do it again. I guess Chris and I learned early the allure, not to mention constant temptation of sin.

As a quick psychological note, some young sinners try to justify smoking by using the excuse that "cigarettes made me sick" and "I will never smoke again." For my readers who might be curious, let me put your mind at ease — cigarettes did not bother Chris Hammond and me — not one iota! To the contrary, we felt great after smoking a few cigarettes and we felt we were worldly and wise, not to mention cigarettes seemed to stimulate good conversation. Chris and I were good conversationalists.

As was typically the case, I was soon caught and at my mother's instructions my father marched me to the back bedroom where I received my customary whipping. It was not the first or the last time I went to the back bedroom, if you know what I mean.

As everyone knows, we are all deep thinkers in Marion County, especially when properly stimulated.

Over the years, I snuck off behind the barn and smoked cigarettes with most, if not all, the youth of South Pittsburg's proper society, which included Mike Quarles, Dick Ryan, Billy Wynne, Phil Colquette, Dava Jane Raulston, Holly Raulston, Debbie Kirkpatrick, and Jane Hamilton, just to name a few and to get their names in my book as fellow sinners.

I smoked my last cigarette in 1984. I thought cigarettes were downright tasty to the very end.

If I live to be 90 years old, on my 90th birthday I plan to go to a tobacco shop and buy a case of Pall Mall cigarettes, non-filtered. I guess when I am 90 years old, Sharon will hopefully overlook one more eccentric characteristic I have developed.

Nothing has ever been better for deep thought or for a stimulating conversation than a "cold one" and a Pall Mall cigarette. As everyone knows, we are all deep thinkers in Marion County, especially when properly stimulated. When smoking cigarettes and talking to my compatriots, I thought Marion County was the intellectual capital of the world.

With the above background in mind, we fast forward 50 years by which time the Congress of the United States of America finally caught on to "Claude Swafford's clarion call of alarm that cigarettes are a dangerous sin." Congress was not particularly concerned about the sin aspect of smoking; however, there were health issues.

I remember one day, in particular, the U.S. Congress subpoenaed all the presidents and chief executive officers of the major tobacco companies to testify. I direct your attention to the fact that these men all had world class educations, all were extremely rich and these men did not smoke themselves. Simply stated, these fellows were all members of what we commonly refer to (in Marion County) as rich folks or respected members of proper society.

During congressional testimony (taken under oath), Congressman Henry Waxman (with whom I am not typically sympathetic) asked the question whether cigarettes and/or tobacco are addictive. Every tobacco official testified under oath without exception and without hesitation that cigarettes were "not addictive."

While I would never want to be judgmental, I can say with absolute certainty that the testimony of the tobacco officials was a "bold face lie" not to mention perjury.

If I had been the Attorney General I would have indicted all those who made such representations that tobacco is not addictive on grounds of perjury before Congress.

Every year in the U.S. 443,000 people die as a result of tobacco related complications while another 8.6 million people suffer from tobacco related complications. Every year health costs reach a staggering $193 billion. I can assure anybody and I can state with the certainty of the sun rising in the morning "tobacco is addictive," particularly Pall Mall non-filters.

LIFE'S LESSON:

As you go through life — BEWARE! Those who are well-educated and well-financed are not above lying. Proper society will lie in a second without hesitation and without remorse.

Keep Your Hands Off the Women, Spouses and Children

By Graham Swafford

*T*he life lesson I present in this feature takes all the will power and self-control most humans can muster. There are some who don't have the self-control, the will power or the inclination to follow the rule in this "Life's Lesson." This lesson, when followed, will be of untold benefit not to mention will inevitably save those who understand and follow the rule from untold grief down the road.

So here are the facts:

Periodically in life there will be people "who just don't like you" or people "you don't like." This is code for "we hate each other's guts." Mutual dislike happens to the best of us, both saints and sinners — get over it! In my view, if you don't have someone who dislikes you, then you aren't doing anything.

> *I am not unmindful of the Biblical directive about forgiveness (which I try to follow most of the time when convenient),*
>
> *if for no other reason, hatred is unhealthy.*

Visceral dislike and/or hatred reminds me of a line in one of LeAnn Womack's songs:

"A regular Nobel Peace Prize winner ... But I really hate her ... I'll think of a reason later ..."

I am not unmindful of the Biblical directive about forgiveness (which I try to follow most of the time when convenient), if for no other reason, hatred is unhealthy.

I have discovered when you are disliked or when you dislike someone always treat the spouses of these people graciously with kindness and solicitude. More important, absolutely bend over backwards to be friendly, helpful, supportive, generous, kind and gracious to the children of those who hate your guts.

When one vents their vitriol on spouses and/or children (particularly children), a bad situation — no matter how justified — always gets worse. Trust me, *nothing* gets a person into trouble faster than mistreating someone else's kid even when mistreatment is deserved. Taking your dislike out on someone's child shows no class. Mistreating someone else's child for whatever reason will haunt you and somewhere down the road, when you least expect it, there will be a price to pay.

Last, but not least, people who hate your guts are absolutely befuddled when you are extremely nice to their spouses and children (particularly their children).

I learned the above lesson early.

LIFE'S LESSON:

Keep your hatred off the spouses and children. Be particularly nice to the children of those who hate your guts. Kindness (especially to the children) will leave those who dislike you absolutely bewildered and befuddled.

I stress — "Keep your hands off the wives and kids."

Lessons of a Heavenly Father — From an Earthly Father

By Dave Daffron
Jasper, Tenn.

*M*y eyes open, and in the house I smell bacon frying and also fresh coffee. I swing my feet over the edge of the bed and head toward the kitchen to have a bowl of oatmeal, some bacon, and make believe coffee with my father. There, I see my father sitting at the kitchen table doing what he does every morning before work — reading his Bible and of course, praying. My father had to be at work early, and he would get up and get breakfast going. Mother worked too, but she didn't have to be there as early as my father. So it was here that I learned the stories of Shadrach, Meshach and Abednego, of Joseph and his coat of many colors, of Noah and the Ark, and Jesus with the little boy's lunch.

> *He was never afraid to say he loved me.*

It was at this time that my faith was grounded. It was a time with a father who would so eagerly teach lessons, not only from the Bible but life itself. I remember asking him why he got up early to read the Bible and talk with God. His answer was simple: "Because I need courage to face the day ahead."

I think fondly now of those times with my father. His big hands and arms would hold me, and he would say, "I love you a bushel and a peck and hug around your neck." He was never afraid to say he loved me. He didn't have to say it, I felt it. His love, he would tell me, was strong, but not as strong as my Heavenly Father's. As a boy, I never quite understood, but still his message was received.

Like so many young men, I wandered away from church, but there was always something drawing me back — the memories of an earthly father telling me how much my Heavenly Father loves me and sharing stories of that love.

Many years have gone by since those boyhood days in the Eastdale section of Chattanooga. My earthly father has been with his Heavenly Father for over a decade, and not a day goes by that I don't remember those lessons from my childhood.

LIFE'S LESSON:
Though we may not understand at first, a good example
and strong love will eventually get the message across.

A Good Plan

By Graham Swafford

*T*he summer I graduated from high school, my father got me a job with Jack Steele, a local contractor in South Pittsburg, Tenn.

I should have expected a conspiracy.

The first day on the job, we were working on the Mary Anderson house on Holly Avenue. Mrs. Anderson was an old-line, dignified, first grade teacher at South Pittsburg Elementary School — a great gal — a memorable gal. Mrs. Anderson also had blue hair.

The construction problem on Mrs. Anderson's house was obvious even to the inexperienced. Moisture had gotten behind the concrete front porch and a portion of the sub-floor had rotted. The concrete porch had to be removed to make the necessary repairs. The problem was that simple.

> *I should have expected a conspiracy.*

Within two minutes after arriving on the job for my first day of work, Mr. Steele handed me a sledge hammer and after pointing to the concrete porch uttered the memorable phrase "Go to it son — bust it up." Mr. Steele then drove away with a content smile on his face leaving me on the job.

About three hours later, Mr. Steele returned to the scene. To say the least, it had already been a long day and I was far from finished. I was worn out, not to mention I had blisters on my hands.

Mr. Steele walked up to me and handed me a set of gloves and told me "keep up the good work you are doing a great job" then he happily climbed back into his pickup truck.

As Mr. Steele was putting his truck into gear to drive away he looked over at me once again, smiled and then uttered these unforgettable words: "Son, by the time I get through with you this summer, you will want to go to law school."

<u>LIFE'S LESSON:</u>
A good plan well-funded and executed beats genius every time. I guess Jack and my father had a plan.

He Will Sell You Out in a Second

By Graham Swafford

I will give you some legal and political advice.

I don't hold myself out as being a world-class expert on anything, however with some modesty I can say I do know a little bit about lawyers. My mother, my father, my sister, my brother-in-law and my daughter are all lawyers and I know a bunch more lawyers.

> *I am of the opinion the two professions facing the greatest temptations in the world are lawyers and preachers.*

I have known about lawyering all my life. When I grew up, I thought the only math a person needed to know was how to divide by three.

I am of the opinion the two professions facing the greatest temptations in the world are lawyers and preachers.

In the 35 years I have practiced law, I have come to the conclusion that the lawyers I have met are the finest, most intelligent, honorable people I have ever known. Not to editorialize too much, but lawyers were writing the Declaration of Independence and the Bill of Rights when doctors were drawing blood with leeches.

I would rather be with a group of lawyers than with anybody on the planet. I direct your attention to the fact that typically it is lawyers who make the greatest contribution in politics, public service, etc., just to name a few.

If I had to do it again I would be a lawyer. I will never forget the day my mother called and told me I had been accepted into law school. The remembrance of that phone call is touching to this day. The truth is, my mother had doubts about whether I would get into law school.

Having fully extolled the divine virtues of lawyers, I acknowledge that periodically I hear people say "my lawyer sold me out" or "his lawyer sold him out." Reba McEntire sang a song referring to a "backwoods Southern lawyer" (corrupt lawyer) and a "judge with bloodstains on his hands" (corrupt judge).

I will give you my experience — I have not seen many corrupt lawyers in my life, but I have witnessed lapses in judgment. I have never (I repeat — never) seen a truly corrupt judge in my life.

<u>LIFE'S LESSON:</u>

So I make the following life lesson which applies not only to lawyers but everybody and every profession, particularly to lawyers and politicians:

The lawyer you think you can buy is the lawyer who will sell you out in a second — Don't kid yourself!

You can take this lesson to the bank.

Don't Keep a Record of Wrongs
By Dr. Nell W. Mohney
Chattanooga, Tenn.

The incident happened on a warm spring afternoon when I was in high school. Yet, the memory is as fresh as a budding rose. In the art of living, it is significant because of the good advice my mother gave me. Her wise counsel has held me in good stead through the intervening years.

My best friend in high school was a girl named Mildred. She was smart, athletic, popular and active in our church's youth program. I not only liked her, but admired her as well. We spent weekends at each other's homes, shared our innermost secrets and cheered each other in our varied activities. It was a wonderful friendship that has endured through the years, but not without its ups and downs.

> *Revenge is sweet to a high school sophomore.*

It was at one of the down times that mother gave me her gem of wisdom. One of the attributes that I admired most about Mildred was her zest for living. She was action oriented, and being around her was never, never "dullsville."

As often happens with such highly motivated people, Mildred had a volatile temper. In one of her flare-ups, she said some things that really hurt me. That afternoon, amid my own angry tears, I told my mother about the incident, but I didn't stop with that one incident. Suddenly, I had instant recall. I remembered every bad thing, both real and imagined, that Mildred had done since our friendship begun.

Listening patiently until I ran out of steam, my mother said: "Nell, you don't keep a record of wrongs. It's fine for you to deal with your feelings, to have a confrontation with Mildred, even to end the friendship, but don't keep a record of wrongs. It will make you bitter."

Luxuriating in comfortable feelings of self pity and being victimized, I didn't like hearing my mother's advice. Revenge is sweet to a high school sophomore. Even in adult life I've learned that revenge, though destructive, can be enjoyable.

My mother's words, however, didn't miss their mark. When I have been tempted to keep score in marriage, as a minister's wife or in friendship, the sentence "don't keep a record of wrongs" has flashed across my mind like a neon sign.

Perhaps all of this was brought to my attention when I met two women on an out-of-town speaking engagement. Both were in their late 50s, both were widows, and both had three grown children. Beyond that, the similarities ceased. The first lady came to talk with me about her unhappiness. She didn't have to tell me she was unhappy. Her posture, her mannerisms, her facial expression all communicated dejection. When I looked at her face, I remembered that Dr. E. Stanley Jones once said: "The face that you have from birth to age 25 is the face you were born with; the face you have from 25 to 50 is the face you earn; and the face that you have from 50 on is the face you deserve."

Immediately upon being seated, she began her recital of complaints. She said: "My husband had to go and die on me just when we had some freedom for travel" (her exact words); "My children don't love or take care of me"; "My friends never invite me out to dinner." Suddenly I realized that my mother was right. This woman's record of wrongs had made her miserable and bitter.

The other woman was one I had heard about before I met her. Words like positive, affirming, radiant were used to describe her. My good friend had told me two different situations this lady had lived through with good grace — a period of alcoholism by her husband, and several years of serious rebellion by a teenage son. She inadvertently gave the secret of her radiance when in a small group she said: "I've learned how to deal with difficulties by facing them, forgiving and moving forward through the power of Christ." In other words, she had burned her records of wrongs.

<u>LIFE'S LESSON:</u>
Keeping a record of wrongs will only lead to misery and bitterness. Forget revenge and instead face your difficulties, forgive, and move on.

Lesson 23

The Christmas Story
and the Suggestion of Reading the Bible

By Graham Swafford

arth Brooks sings a song about having "Friends in Low Places." I'm not sure we have many friends in high places, but I can state with certainty Sharon and I, Little Graham and Shelton have friends who have "spotted pasts," if you know what I mean.

Several years ago, I represented a gentleman (his name will remain unmentioned due to sophistication and sensitivity) who I guess had the "spotted past."

Typically, my wife and children have not enjoyed the pleasure of meeting my criminal clients; however, this particular criminal client was different and we all just became good friends. My friend would come to the house, do yardwork for us, etc. Ignoring a full and complete review of our friends' extensive rap sheet, we were all completely comfortable with this client. To this day the kids still ask about this fellow. Our friend has called the house from the penitentiary just to talk with Sharon and me.

My client was always being sent to jail for something which the Swaffords chose to give a blind eye. Perhaps the Swaffords are just not members of proper society (or so I have been told lately).

Those unfamiliar with the legal profession (or at least those unfamiliar with country lawyering) will be interested to learn that after December 17 of each year the law business sort of winds down and we have plenty of time on our hands for contemplation. I suppose people would rather pay for Christmas (or anything else for that matter) over the holidays than paying for a lawyer.

On one particular Christmas, our good friend was once again incarcerated in the Marion County Jail for some minor, but much ballyhooed indiscretion.

I would be remiss if I did not point out that Sherry Shelton, the local district attorney (who by the way is rather likeable but at times can be a little unforgiving) had relentlessly prosecuted my old friend. Sherry Shelton sometimes goes overboard prosecuting the misunderstood as was the case involving my friend on the particular Christmas I am recounting. For academic integrity, my readers will be interested to know Sherry Shelton graduated from college with highest honors majoring in psychology. I don't think the psychology degree did Sherry any good; however, she remains extremely bright, perceptive and likeable. I repeat — she just has the proclivity to go overboard.

As I was sitting at my desk over the Christmas holiday, contemplating the rest of my day, I picked up my dictaphone and dictated a motion to the court requesting a furlough to allow me to pick up my friend from the Marion County jail and take him out to for a Christmas luncheon.

I guess I was trying to be a witness.

When I first presented the motion to Judge Clifford Layne for approval, I was uncertain whether he would actually sign the order. My guess is that Judge Layne was so completely confounded or knocked senseless by the unusual, if not preposterous request, that he signed or approved the furlough order prior to any contemplation.

We all know what would have happened if Judge Layne had given the motion a millisecond of thought or if Sherry Shelton (who by the way was not in the Christmas spirit) had gotten wind of my request.

I went down to the Marion County jail and picked up my friend who was delighted to see me at Christmas time. We then retired to the Western Sizzlin Steakhouse on I-24 for our "Christmas luncheon."

Our old friend picked out the most expensive meal on the menu; however, I expressed no objection. After all, we were not at the Mountain City Club.

During our luncheon, I tried to impart a little Christmas cheer and give a little advice to my old buddy. I gently suggested to my friend that it would appear to me he had a lot of time on his hands as an inmate at the Marion County jail and I would recommend that he read the Bible from cover to cover and "draw his own conclusions." I guess I was trying to be a witness.

What a disaster! I will think twice before I try to witness again. With the "read the Bible suggestion" my old friend proceeded to launch off on a diatribe about the Bible, the church, church folk, sin, drinking, sex, the world is unfair, hypocrisy in general, and on and on. You just had to be there to get the full illogical blast I received from my old friend.

My old friend then made representations about religion that had absolutely no Biblical basis and/or academic foundation. His views were stunningly inaccurate not to mention misstated, if not possibly dangerous.

Shortly thereafter, to my great relief, I took my friend back to the jail and dropped him off wishing him a Merry Christmas. I then proceeded home to Sharon with great sadness in my heart. I had fumbled an opportunity to witness.

LIFE'S LESSON:
At one time in your life read the Bible from cover to cover then draw your own conclusions.

*Note: I would also like to suggest reading the Bill of Rights — another document nobody seems to have read lately.

Life Is About Levels

By Graham Swafford

*S*everal years ago, I took my family to Washington, D.C., at which time I was admitted to practice before the Supreme Court of the United States of America. I was pretty full of myself. I'm not sure my family recognized the significance of the occasion; however, we all had a great time. As I was sitting there, I saw other people being admitted to practice before the Supreme Court and quickly it dawned on me that there were those doing far more important stuff than I.

> *Quickly it dawned on me that there were those doing far more important stuff than I.*

Fast forwarding to a couple of years ago, I was in East Tennessee learning to fly an airplane. I was in a rented Cessna 172 and while the aircraft had a degree of air worthiness (it got off the ground) it was a little drafty not to mention shaky.

Notwithstanding the problems of my rented aircraft, I was "proud of myself." On this particular afternoon, the community (where I was taking my lesson) had suffered the loss of an individual who, in a very honorable fashion, had accumulated great wealth and been extremely generous to his community. As I was standing on the airport ramp I saw exotic airplanes come in and land (I assume for the gentleman's funeral) the kind and degree of which I had only read about.

Over the years, I can give hundreds, if not thousands, of stories similar to the above. Simply stated, life is about levels. Just when you think you're doing pretty well there are always those who are doing better. There is always someone out there quicker, richer, faster, more intelligent, or better looking.

LIFE'S LESSON:
Short and simple: Life is about levels. There are always those above you and if by chance you reach the pinnacle, you will not be there for long.
Levels apply to everything and everyone.

He Ain't No Deacon

By John Hewgley
South Pittsburg, Tenn.

*T*here are lessons learned as a child that teach you the right thing to do or give you an example of what not to do. Many of my life lessons from those I looked up to were lessons on what not to do. So here is my lesson:

My brother Billy and I worked hard from the day mother let Bill Hewgley take us away from her apron strings. We worked at his woodworking shop, at his greenhouse, at his furniture store, on the farm, hauling slop from the high school and hospital to his hogs — just to name a few things we did all our young lives. Occasionally some people in town would need work done or need to borrow dad's truck and he would send us with his truck to do the work. I guess Billy and I were the original "2 Boys and a Truck." We hauled hay, we hauled fertilizer, we hauled hogs, we hauled shrubbery for the housing projects, we hauled everything that he told us to haul. But on one particular weekend he loaned us and the truck out to "The Deacon."

It was like the horses knew we were coming and wanted us to really appreciate the aroma, heat and texture of fresh manure.

It seemed that the Deacon had decided he wanted to plant some rose bushes at his home and needed a truck and some day laborers. Billy and I were dispatched at about 14 and 12 years old. We were young, but old enough to drive dad's '49 Chevy pickup truck downtown to the Deacon's house. When we got there our first job was to dig four grave size square holes in the yard for the roses. That took us most of the morning and finally about noon we headed out to John Price's stables in Jasper for the secret ingredient for the roses ... horse dung! The Deacon wanted to put three feet of this stuff in the bottom of each grave before he planted his roses. He drove dad's truck and took us to Jasper where Billy and I shoveled manure until it was running over the sides of the bed. John Price let him have the best stuff because it was still wet and steaming when we shoveled it out of the stalls. It was like the horses knew we were coming and wanted us to really appreciate the aroma, heat and texture of fresh manure. Maybe you think that I linger too long on the description of our cargo but it is important that you visualize this load to understand the lesson that I learned about two o'clock in the afternoon when we were driving back to deliver our load.

The Deacon was driving Billy, me and the manure from Jasper to South Pittsburg. We had to drive through Kimball and as we approached Dixie Lee Junction, the Deacon looked up and saw a black man dressed in his finest clothes, who was heading to town for a Saturday night, standing on the side of the road near the old Stucky's store. The Deacon looked at Billy and me and yelled: "If that Nigger thumbs me I'm going to pick him up!" I was astonished at what I was hearing from such a well-respected pillar of the community. Language like that was never allowed in our home. The black man raised his arm and stuck out his thumb and the Deacon quickly pulled over. The stranger I recognized as being one of the Gaines men that lived just past us in Battle Creek ran up to the passenger side of the truck where I was sitting with the window down and grabbed the handle to open the door and jump in. At that moment the Deacon looked over Billy and me to the black man and said: "No Nigger, you're not riding up front with us, you get in the back!" The black man looked at the Deacon and then looked at the steaming manure and with terrible shame said: "Naw Sir, I thinks I catch me another ride."

What did I learn that day? People can be cruel and heartless. So when I saw a deacon acting that way even as a young boy I thought: "I just saw what he did to that man and he ain't no Deacon!" The Christ that my momma taught Billy and me about doesn't accept that kind of treatment of his other creations. God made blacks in his image too! I am a child of the south and I am sure that I have shown prejudice as well but if I have ever let myself treat anyone like that then may God have mercy on my soul because I don't deserve mercy.

Sorry, Mr. Gaines … I wish I had told the Deacon to get out of my dad's truck and walk home by himself. Billy and I would have gladly shoveled that manure on my dad's garden because the Deacon did not deserve roses.

LIFE'S LESSON:
Some people, even so-called "pillars of the community,"
will show you what not to do by their example.

Lesson 26

More Advice for Young Lawyers

By Graham Swafford

As lawyers fade into old age approaching dotage, we feel compelled to give advice to young, impressionable lawyers, who are just getting started.

Here is the reality: I am of the opinion there is a group of clients who think that the most brilliant lawyer in the world is the attorney who is telling them exactly what they want to hear. These folks simply do not want to hear the truth — they want to hear what they want to hear.

> *There is a group of clients who think that the most brilliant lawyer in the world is the attorney who is telling them exactly what they want to hear.*

I have interviewed prospective clients and when I told them what they wanted to hear they looked at me with such a glow on their faces you would think they have just spoken to Socrates or the Divine. On the other hand, I have pointed out obvious perils to prospective clients and they stormed out of my office making less than complimentary comments to my long-suffering, dependable secretary, Brandy Pruitt, proclaiming as they exit the front door, "We will go to Chattanooga for a lawyer."

Let me give a warning to young lawyers about four different types of prospective clients which an attorney needs to treat with particular skepticism — every time!

The *first* type of client a young lawyer should be careful about is the type that comes in and proclaims at least four times "I want you to tell me the truth." After practicing law for 35 years, I have discovered when a prospective client tells you repeatedly "I want you to tell me the truth" such is simply code language for "I want you to sunshine my posterior and tell me what I want to hear." No whopper is too big for these type clients.

I gently point out you will have real problems with clients in this group when you can't deliver the results they desired. I repeat — "real problems"!

The *second* type of prospective clients I would like to warn young lawyers about is the type that comes in and right out of the barrel starts saying "I am a great, long-time friend of your parents whom I think the world of (along with the rest of your family) and I have a simple matter I want you to handle."

Prospective clients in this group then repeat what great, long-lasting friends they have been with the family. Amazingly, more times than not, I have never heard of these lifelong friends.

I have discovered when prospective clients pull the "long-time, great friends

63

of your parents" line, this is code language for "this legal matter is going to be too complicated, there is no reasonable resolution, these clients will be very demanding and last but not least, these prospective clients (or lifelong old friends, however you look at it) do not plan to pay much of a fee, if any."

Be careful about these clients.

There is a *third* type of prospective clients young lawyers should be aware of and these are the ones who come in and tell you how "honest" they are. My experience is when people come in and tell me how "honest" they are (particularly when they are wearing fake Rolex watches), then "hold on to your wallet and make sure there is nothing valuable sitting around your office that can be stolen." Typically when those in this group come in and tell you for the fourth time how "honest" they are, you should get ready. More important get your fee up front from this group. Finally I would be remiss if I did not point out that you should beware of the always dangerous "recent converts."

The *fourth* group of prospective clients that young lawyers need to be careful about are those who come in and say "Well, I was going to take this case over to Jim Neal* in Nashville (or whoever happens to be the most famous, most expensive lawyer in the country, at the time), but I thought I would give you a chance." Those in this group then ask with a fake look of curiosity "Do you think you can handle a case like this or do I need to go see Jim Neal (or whoever is famous at the time)?" When a client comes in with the "Jim Neal" line, this is typically code language for "I'm stupid. I can't afford Jim Neal (or whoever). I can't even get an appointment with Jim Neal (or whoever). Typically in this type of situation, the statute of limitations is about to run or there is a horrible undisclosed problem with the case. Young lawyers should definitely watch out for this type client.

If you talk to lawyers who have been around very long, they all (without exception) can tell horror stories about cases they have been snookered into taking and miles down the road (not to mention thousands of dollars later) they made the agonizing statement "How in the world did I get myself involved in this case?"

LIFE'S LESSON:

To young lawyers: Learn to say no! Learn to say no often!
More often than not, the most important lawsuit a lawyer
has is the one the lawyer had the intelligence, not to mention
common sense, to turn down. Lawyers, both young and old,
should all learn how to just say "no"!

Note: I have even had folks tell me they had just talked to Jim Neal before coming to see me. Jim Neal has been dead for several years. I was looking forward to seeing Jim in Marion County — it would be sort of like the second coming.

Lesson 27

Unexpected Lesson

By Graham Swafford

*S*everal years ago, I took my daughter to Washington, D.C., where we attended a pro-life rally at the Washington Monument on the Capital Mall. Obviously, I made a great effort to leave an impression on my impressionable child.

It would be an understatement to say the rally was passionate, if not emotional, and I thought memorable. This was a real father-daughter trip. We had a great time.

I knew I had really made a life-altering impression on my daughter, which she would carry for life.

Several years later, my daughter and I were discussing the trip to Washington and to my horror I discovered that she had gotten a "little confused" to say the least. My daughter thought that I had taken her to a "Pro-Choice Rally." My misguided daughter then opined she was pro-choice and then happily reminded me that on this fun-filled trip to Washington the high point of the trip, as she remembered it, was buying fake Rolex watches on the street. My daughter then beamed when she recounted she could still remember how to tell the difference between a real Rolex and a fake Rolex — a skill not enjoyed by many of her friends, especially at the Girls' Preparatory School — a talent for which she is still proud.

> *...to my horror I discovered that she had gotten a 'little confused' to say the least.*

What a shock! Apparently my daughter not only does not adopt my pro-life views, but the sole impression I left on my impressionable child dealt with buying fake Rolexes.

<u>LIFE'S LESSON:</u>

Be careful what you do — in all probability you are not sending the message to your child and/or children you think you are sending.

Crandel McNabb

By Billy Watkins
Kimball, Tenn.

ne of the first individuals I met when we moved to Marion County was Crandel McNabb. I quickly realized that "Mr. Mac," as he was affectionately called, was a special person indeed, someone from whom I could learn.

Mr. Mac was not a man who threw his weight around, nor was he forceful or overbearing. He was rather quiet and unassuming, but inside he was all man, and he used that quality to help young men develop into men. You see, Mr. Mac was a Boy Scout leader. However, he was not just your run-of-the-mill leader, he took an interest in the boys who came his way. He was a leader who tried to bring out the best in each and every young man. He looked for ways to draw out the potentials which he saw in every boy, and then worked with them to develop those potentials. He wanted the boys to have skills of scouting as well as skills for life, and he worked toward these ends for years.

> *Greatness is not always achieved in newsworthy deeds; it can be achieved by helping others.*

Mr. Mac did not simply tell boys what to do or how to do it, he helped them attain the necessary skills they needed to accomplish a goal or advance in rank. This he did by working individually with the boys. Mr. Mac also demonstrated this need for personal development. In doing so, he earned every award a scout master could earn; including the Silver Beaver award, the highest in scouting, and the God and Country award.

In this way, he encouraged the scouts to achieve the highest honors they could. The number of Eagle scouts that learned from him demonstrates that several boys learned their lessons very well.

Mr. Mac invested himself in the development of the scouts. He traveled around the country with "his" boys to give them opportunities to see and explore new places, to gain new skills, and to meet scouts from other parts of the U.S. He took them camping, fishing, hiking, and shared his knowledge of the outdoors with "his" boys. Although he only had one son of his own, Mr. Mac had a lot of "sons," and he helped an untold number of boys to grow into men. Perhaps better men than they would be without his direction. While he trained all these young men, he always did so as a Christian gentleman and with a Christian example that the boys could follow. In an age when so many male leaders are coming under question, this is a refreshing quality indeed.

Mr. Mac will never appear on the cover of some major news magazine as a national hero, but he lives, as a hero, in the hearts of the young men whose lives he so positively touched. He not only used his skills with scouts, he also used them in developing leaders in Christ's church in which he loved and served for many years. Greatness is not always achieved in newsworthy deeds; it can be achieved by helping others, and this is the way Mr. Mac achieved greatness. This is the wonderful legacy he leaves to all of us. His is a legacy of helping others; the investment of self and time in others. If more of us did the same, this would be a much better world. Therein lays true greatness.

This brings us to the life lesson of Crandel McNabb.

LIFE'S LESSON:

Time invested in helping others develop is one of the best investments anyone can make in life. It lives on in the next generation.

Thanks for teaching me this important lesson Mr. Mac!

True Friends

By Graham Swafford

The next "Life's Lesson" does not come with a story, BUT don't be confused — I can give thousands of first-hand examples on this lesson.

As a person goes through life (particularly when one enjoys some prominence), people refer to them as a "great and lifelong, personal friend." Everybody wants to be intimate friends of the rich and famous. Nobody wants to admit knowing the bankrupt and incarcerated. I know very few people who have the spine, character or fidelity to go see an old friend in the penitentiary.

> *I have so many self-proclaimed, close, personal friends you would think I had graduated from charm school.*

If I had a nickel for every person who told me how much they thought of me and then proclaimed they were my "lifelong, close, personal friend," I would rent a fleet of jets and take all of my readers to Disneyland and thereafter on a "round-the-world cruise." I have so many self-proclaimed, close, personal friends you would think I had graduated from charm school.

I have no illusions.

Let me give you a "rule of thumb." At the end of your life if you have five people who you can really call a "close friend" then you should consider yourself not only lucky but a "great success."

There are two qualities that I consider in a great friend:

A true friend is loyal! Nothing in the world is more painful (not to mention embarrassing and hurtful) than getting stabbed in the back by someone you thought was a friend.

A true friend will call you and give you *bad news* that you don't want to hear. In my view, nothing is more treasured than a friend who has my back or will call me to deliver bad news.

LIFE'S LESSON:

About true friendship: At the end of your life, don't expect more than five, true friends.

The two most important characteristics of a true friend are loyalty and willingness to call you and give you bad, unwanted news. Always remember there is a giant *difference between a true friend and an acquaintance.*

The Importance of Childhood Security

By Graham Swafford

*G*rowing up on Contour Avenue in South Pittsburg, Tenn., our family's closest and dearest neighbors were Chick and Ali Jane Raulston and their three daughters — Dava Jane, Jody and Lynn.

I don't mean to brag about my neighbors, but the Raulstons were the most charming people on the planet. Nobody had a greater combination of passion and humor than Joe (Chick) Raulston — "The nut did not fall far from the tree." I always thought Lynn had traits of her mother; Jody had many of the traits of her dad and Dava Jane had a combination of her parents.

In addition to being funny and having the greatest personalities on the planet the Raulston girls were pretty good looking, however I mention this only because my readers expect academic accuracy in my book.

Now the Swaffords of Contour Avenue were fairly personable, but we were nothing to really crow about.

When guests visited the Swaffords, after a couple hours, we liked to send them on their way relying upon the old adage "guests are like fish — after they have been sitting around for a while they start to smell."

The Raulstons, on the other hand, were the most charming, entertaining folks in the entire world. In addition to a steady stream of locals who came to enjoy the Raulston's companionship and the allure of the Raulston girls, people would come from miles away to visit the Raulston family. The Swaffords were always a little amazed. Nobody — and I repeat "nobody" wanted to visit the Swaffords for any extended time.

At any rate, I think it is fairly obvious we have to this day high regard for the Raulstons.

The best thing about growing up on Contour Avenue in South Pittsburg, Tenn., was the sense of security. Everybody cared about everybody.

I remember once as a very young boy, I was alone at home with my maternal grandmother who suffered from what was probably a nervous breakdown. The occasion could have been very traumatic for a young boy; however no big deal — I immediately dashed next door to Ali Jane Raulston who came over and calmed my agitated grandmother. The situation could have gotten out of hand.

I remember one time Chick got mad at Dava Jane. Dava Jane took off and

> *I had finally relaxed for more deep thought and suddenly slipped into the commode where I became securely stuck.*

Chick started chasing her. Dava Jane dashed to our house and my mother hid Dava Jane in the closet. A few minutes later Chick came busting in asking where Dava Jane was and my mother responded, "We have not seen her, but we will keep our eyes open."

The stories are endless. I remember one night in particular, as a young man, I retreated to the bathroom to answer "nature's call" where I enjoyed contemplative thought on "the throne."

After a long struggle (if you know what I mean) I had finally relaxed for more deep thought and suddenly slipped into the commode where I became securely stuck.

I screamed for my mother and sister who quickly arrived on the scene providing no assistance whatsoever. I was getting a little scared. Just in the nick of time the Raulstons were summoned for assistance and arrived in force. I will never forget Jody and Dava Jane's gleeful expression as they stared at my plight from the door of the bathroom.

Not to carry a grudge after all these years, but to this day I am still annoyed at Dava Jane and Jody's unrestrained delight, not to mention lack of sympathy.

Ali Jane pulled and tugged for a few minutes then, being the practical woman she is, got some Vaseline and after a liberal application I popped out no worse for the wear.

This brings me to "Life's Lesson," which I hope conveys an expression of gratitude to the Raulstons and our other neighbors on Contour Avenue.

LIFE'S LESSON:

What I learned on Contour Avenue: Nothing is more important for a young child than the safety and security of a safe and secure neighborhood and the knowledge that somebody cares and thinks you and your family are the most important people in the world.

The Swaffords extend our gratitude.

*Note: For those disbelievers out there, I promise you the above story is very true.

illustration by Norris Hall

Send Someone My Way

By Jackie Daffron
Jasper, Tenn.

R-r-r-ring! That is the sound which led to a chain of events that impacted my life.

I was sitting at home alone with not a lot to do. Dave and I had decided I would be a "stay-at-home mom" until Misty got old enough to attend school. Well, she was now in school, and I didn't have a job. My teaching degree was in health and physical education, and there were no openings in that area when school started that year. Now it is December, and the phone rang.

There was an opening for a Special Education teacher at the Whiteside Elementary School and the principal wanted me to come interview for the job. I knew nothing about this area but went anyway. When she presented the job description, it sounded like it would be right for me.

God gave me the "gift" of great patience and concern and this special area required both. HE led me to this school.

My classroom was the little stage separated from the kindergarten class by a curtain. There was room enough for my desk and a small table with six chairs, and I loved it!

One of my students was a sweet, little boy whose odor almost made me open the curtain for air. I found out he lived in a house with no heat and at night they would bring in their goats so the family could sleep with them to keep warm. I gathered up some blankets and sent them home with him.

I am hoping that his soul is right with the Lord.

Another child came from an "impossible" home environment. He was sweet and I loved him. He is now on death row for murder. Shortly before the date of his execution, I called the prison chaplain and asked him to talk with "Sam" about God and he assured me he would. I sent a Bible hoping he would read it. He wrote me several letters after that, so I am hoping that his soul is right with the Lord.

"Sally" never talked. After working with her for over a year (and I am not bragging, well maybe just a little), she started talking and, so far as I know, hasn't stopped, even for a breath of air.

In this same school, I had three students from a large family who lived in a school bus. I hope they learned how to read and do math well enough to get into a better environment.

These are just a few of the challenges the first year of teaching brought me. God has sent so many students my way during my 37 years of teaching. He has had His hands in my career all the way. He provided the positions and the experiences in all of them and this all started with a phone call from someone I did not know, to a school I had never heard of, for a job I knew nothing about.

Thank you, Lord.

LIFE'S LESSON:

You never know what God has planned for using your gifts.
Answer the call!

Marriage, Education and Religion
or
Sleeping with Cannibals and Drunk Christians
By Graham Swafford

*M*y next life lesson will constitute an observation. I will not tell a story; however, I have thousands of stories that apply to this "Life's Lesson."

I pose this question: "What does marriage, education and religion have in common?"

I don't mean to brag, but I am an expert on marriage, education and religion.

I don't mean to brag, but I am an expert on marriage, education and religion.

As far as marriage is concerned, I have been married for over 39 years and I have represented hundreds if not several thousand divorce clients. Simply stated, you don't have a story I can't top. I have heard all the stories — he's no good — she's no good — his family's crazy — her family's crazy — he's lazy — she's lazy — he runs around — she runs around … the list is endless!

I know a lot about education. I have had people say their life has been a failure because they had an inadequate education. I have had people tell me that they have enjoyed fame and fortune because they went to big, fancy schools. I have had people come in and tell me they contribute their fame and fortune to the fact that they had to figure it out for themselves.

I don't mean to sound like a great theologian, but I have heard all about religion. I have been told the devil is going to get you if you don't go to church. I have been told church folks are hypocrites. I have been told that the difference between the Episcopalians and the Baptists is that the Episcopalians will say "Hi" to you in the liquor store. Herman Melville once wrote he would rather sleep with a cannibal than a drunk Christian. I repeat I know a lot about religion.

I guess you folks get the idea — I am a world class expert.

LIFE'S LESSON:

When it comes down to marriage, education and religion, you get out of it what you put into it. It is always an individual decision and effort.

Divorce and the 80 Percent Rule

By Graham Swafford

*O*ver the years, I suppose I have represented over 1,000 individuals in divorce cases.

Over the years, I have advised people to get a divorce and later they told me they regretted not following my advice.

Over the years, I have told people they did not need to get a divorce and I have been told later getting a divorce was a mistake and they wished they had followed my advice.

For this life's lesson, I will not try to take credit with being right every time nor will I try to take credit for being wrong every time.

LIFE'S LESSON:

1. If you are young and you are married, without children, and you realize you have made a mistake "fix your problem quick."

2. If you are married to a man who beats you, get a divorce.

3. Eighty percent of the people who get a divorce are no better off five years from the divorce. To the contrary, most times families are worse off after the divorce. Only about 10 percent or 20 percent improve their position by divorce. The kids pay a horrific price.

Lesson 34

Simple Advice

By Charles G. Jenkins Sr.
Jasper, Tenn.

I was raised in Coal City Hollow in South Pittsburg, Tenn., on the Georgia side of the state line. The only road in and out of the Hollow was through Tennessee. The state of Georgia had a deal with Marion County to let the Hollow kids go to school in Marion County. Hence I attended school in New Hope and South Pittsburg.

I was born in 1940 in Rossville, Ga., as the depression was ending and World War II was beginning. Both of these wars greatly influenced my life. To find work my dad's family moved to Rossville to work there and around Chattanooga, Tenn. We stayed on the family farm which consisted of 75 acres. My daddy worked in the mines and in timber all over Tennessee, Georgia and Kentucky. Sometime in 1942 he went to work with TVA at Hales Bar Dam as a truck driver. In 1943 he was drafted into the Army.

After the war daddy started to work in Alton Park at Southern Chemical Cotton Company and worked there until he retired in 1981. Through high school I spent a considerable part of my life in Rossville. My aunts and uncles and grandmas rented from an old lady who drove up once a month and collected rent. She gave them a white receipt and they gave her money. This made an impression on me.

Another thing that influenced my life was the returning servicemen. Without fail they would say "if I had more education I could go places" and they would say "if I had money I would buy real estate." I resolved to do both.

An early commitment to God and his teaching has been the guiding force in my life. I have tried to live my life and conduct my business by Christian principals.

At the age of 13, I told everyone who would listen that I hated being poor and was going to do something about it. By the time I was 16, and after watching many hours of Perry Mason, I decided to be a lawyer. My high school yearbook, in 1959, states "Charles Jenkins, the lawyer" but then the reality of no money hit me.

In 1959, in Marion County, there were basically two classes of people. You either had some money or you did not have money. So getting money to go to college was a problem.

A high school friend, Ronald Carson, and I decided to move to Nashville and go to Falls Business College. Schools did not have guidance counselors and the only encouragement I got was from Mr. Phil Beene, principal, and Mr. Roger Patton. They made a trip to my house in Coal City to inquire of my career plans. They told me that I had scored number four in my class on the final achievement test and was college material and I also had received the highest grade in history. I lasted one semester at Falls Business College. I then joined the Air Force and became an Air Policeman.

We ended the semester with $10.

During my last year in high school, Alaska became a state. In my circle of friends we talked about going to Alaska to homestead. After Air Police School, I volunteered to go to Alaska. I went to Ladd Air Force Base in Fairbanks, Alaska. I enrolled in the University of Alaska for 21 months and then came to Turner Air Force Base in Albany, Ga.

In July 1962, I met my future wife, Alice. We married in December of that year. She was with me for the last eight months of my four-year tour. This was the best time of our 46 years together.

Upon discharge in September of 1963, I enrolled at the University of Chattanooga taking 17 hours. My son, Charles Jenkins Jr. was born halfway through the first semester. We ended the semester with $10.

Somehow, we came up with enough money to finance the next semester. I took 18 hours and made the Dean's List. I then took eight hours in the first summer semester which made me 61 hours.

That fall, I started teaching at Mount Olive School on a temporary teaching certificate. Mount Olive was one of the last one-room schools in Marion County, Tenn. My salary was $341 per month for 10 months. My wife worked at the Handle Factory and we lived pretty well.

The summer of 1965, I worked for Life and Casualty Insurance Company. The fall of 1965, I was promoted to a three teacher school, Pine Hill in the Pocket Community on Whitwell Mountain. I went to school at night and by the summer of 1966 I had 24 semester hours. In June of 1966, I started work as a production supervisor at 3M in Chattanooga, Tenn. That was a very good job, but I still had my dreams of being a lawyer. I finished my work for my bachelor's degree in December 1967. In the fall of 1968, I quit 3M and started operating the Shell station in Kimball, Tenn. I also took the law school admission test and was admitted to the University of Tennessee School of Law for the fall semester of 1969.

My business was going good and I started buying real estate. I also took flying lessons to fly to law school because I did not want to move to Knoxville. I was at law school in the summer of 1970 for one semester but could not move up there because of business and my son started to school.

In 1971, I started to the Nashville School of Law and graduated from there in 1975 and started practicing law. I practiced law for 31 years.

In 1991, my son started practicing law with me. I served 12-plus years as judge.

Charles Jenkins Company provides housing for over 100 Marion County families.

My family has had "a great run."

LIFE'S LESSON:

Follow the Lord, work hard, never quit, get an education and buy real estate.

No Good Deed Goes Unreturned

By Graham Swafford

*Y*ears ago, before the invention of the automobile, interstate highway and airplanes, very few people traveled at all. Those who did travel typically traveled long distances by train and when they arrived at their destinations accommodations were often scarce. It was not at all uncommon for travelers to "bunk up" or all stay in the same room.

I take you to the 1800s. Samuel Clemens a/k/a Mark Twain was the most prominent writer and public speaker in the entire country. Twain's services as a speaker were in tremendous demand. On one particular occasion, Twain was performing a speaking engagement in San Francisco. After a long, cross-country trip to San Francisco by train, Twain arrived at his destination and checked into a hotel room, which he was sharing with another traveling companion.

> *Borrowing a Marion County expression, Twain's friend was 'dog drunk.'*

As evening approached, the gentlemen found themselves at the bar. After "wetting his whistle," Twain told his bunk mate he was going to "retire" early that evening.

Thereafter, Twain retired to his room, went to bed and went to sleep.

Hours (and I mean hours) later, the bunk mate finally appeared back at the room. Borrowing a Marion County expression, Twain's friend was "dog drunk."

Twain looked at his bunk mate and said "Well, where have you been?" to which the bunk mate replied: "You would not believe what happened to me out here." The companion continued: "After you (Twain) returned to the room I ran into a fellow who knew you. It was horrible." The bunk mate then proceeded to tell Twain the fellow he had met did not say a good thing about Twain. He talked the entire night about what a rascal, not to mention, a scoundrel Twain was. Twain's drunken friend made it very clear that not one good thing was said about Mark Twain the entire evening. I repeat — not one good thing.

After a few minutes, Twain looked at his "bunk mate" and in a moment of contemplative thought said "Well, whoever was saying all those bad things about me must have been someone whom I had been particularly nice and done a real favor for at one time — I must have been really nice to him."

LIFE'S LESSON:

No good deed goes unreturned or…

Sometimes a good stabbing in the back comes from unex-pected places and at unexpected times.

---

*Note: I share this lesson, which was told to me by Geoff Post, president of Citizens State Bank.

Silver Bullets

By Graham Swafford

ver the years, I have been involved in politics.

I have known people who have been worthy public servants and have made positive contributions that will effect generations to come. I have known first rate political thugs and crooks who have caused untold damage, not to mention betrayed the public trust.

Public policy and prudent decisions make a difference, regardless of political stripe.

On the Republican side, I am reminded of Abraham Lincoln, Teddy Roosevelt, Dwight D. Eisenhower, Howard Baker, Lamar Alexander, Bill Brock, Zack Wamp and Ronald Reagan. I personally thought Richard Nixon was a very competent president. I supported Nixon to the bitter end, a belief I hold without apology or regret.

The public is a fickle animal for both good and bad.

On the Democratic side, I always admired Woodrow Wilson, Al Gore Jr. and Franklin D. Roosevelt. I point out that had it not been for the good judgment and prudent handling of the Cuban Missile Crisis by John F. Kennedy, society as we know it could have been obliterated in a nuclear war.

There have been other political leaders. In particular, I admired Winston Churchill and Margaret Thatcher and now that I am being generous, I think Hillary has a few redeeming qualities.

The above comment brings me to the point of this lecture. All politicians have a certain limited number of "silver bullets." Some politicians have more bullets than others. I repeat there are a limited number of bullets.

No matter how honorable the politician, no matter how great the vision of the politician, no matter how crazy the politician, no matter how solid the judgment of the politician, sooner, if not later, the politician's "silver bullets" will all be discharged and the political career ends.

The public is a fickle animal for both good and bad. I have happily witnessed the above rule and I have witnessed the above rule with tremendous sadness.

LIFE'S LESSON:
All politicians have a certain number of "Silver Bullets."

Some politicians, for whatever reason, have more bullets than others. It is important for a politician to know when all of his/her silver bullets have been discharged, at which time the politician should declare victory and go to the house.

Note: I have known very few politicians who could recognize when the bullets are fired and it is time to go to the house after declaring victory.

Second note: My old friend, Jane Wilson Dawkins, refers to the above lesson as staying too long at the dance. Same identical lesson — just another name.

Security / Self-Confidence

By Dava Jane Raulston Quarles
South Pittsburg, Tenn.

*W*hen Graham asked me to contribute to his book on Life's Lessons he specifically told me not to write about the Swaffords. I will ignore his instructions.

The luck of growing up on Contour Avenue in South Pittsburg, Tenn., can't be overstated.

I cannot express my gratitude for the good judgment of my mother. Nothing in my life has been more important than the closeness I have enjoyed with my sisters, Lynn and Jody. Our father taught us to laugh and dance. We had a memorable neighborhood. Howard and Claude Swafford were our next door neighbors. Howard and Claude were our extended parents and Chick and Allie Jane were the Swafford kids' extended parents.

The stories are endless. In moments of great crisis the Swafford kids would come to get my parents and when we were in peril we would go to the Swaffords.

The Swaffords seemed to have an urge to express their views on all topics regardless of their knowledge on the subject.

I remember one day, in particular, Graham and Claudia were at home with their grandmother who suffered an emotional collapse. Without hesitation, Graham came to get my mother — the crisis was averted without damage.

I remember one time my father got mad at me so I ran next door and Claude hid me in the closet.

I can never forget the night Graham got stuck in the toilet, my mother was called to extract him.

When I was in high school, Howard would drop Graham and me off at school. About all I can say is the Swaffords were a little bit different. Every morning I would go to their house, walk into the kitchen to the smell of bacon and eggs, the paper spread across the table and typically the Swaffords were in the middle of some type of discussion. Peace and harmony did not always prevail. Everything was discussed. The Swaffords seemed to have an urge to express their views on all topics regardless of their knowledge on the subject. To this day I know there was more talking than listening. What a great way to start my day.

The stories of good times and the laughter are endless. I remember round table devotions. I remember the time Claude let the car roll off the hill. My parents were invited over that night for dinner at which time Howard was told of another wreck.

To hear them talk you would have thought all of our wars were fought and won single handedly by Howard and my dad.

Over the decades and over the generations our relationship remains close. Claude and Howard worked so hard to provide a beautiful lawn for our wedding. Mike and I are grateful.

When my youngest daughter, Bailey, got married, Graham and Shelton shuttled guests to and from the reception. Shelton stole the show. A few months later, Mike and I shuttled guests at Shelton's wedding reception.

My father and Howard worked together for years in the American Legion. To hear them talk you would have thought all of our wars were fought and won single handedly by Howard and my dad.

Over the years, dad and Howard worked on Girls and Boys State. Years after my father passed away, our daughter Bailey and Shelton (Graham and Sharon's daughter) were elected to be Girls State Representatives from their schools the same year. I know Howard was proud. Chick would have been incredibly proud. The fact that these girls were able to participate together made a statement of the close bond that has lasted through the generations.

LIFE'S LESSONS:
Good friends who are an extension of your family do so much to add to a child's sense of confidence and security.

Dava Jane Raulston taught school for over 30 years in the Marion County School System. Dava Jane and her husband live in the Battlecreek Community of Marion County on property owned by the family for generations. The next generation has already connected.

Sam Bob Raulston

By Graham Swafford

W hen I graduated from law school, I had the pleasure of practicing law with my father, and with Sam Bob Raulston and F. Nat Brown.

I'm not certain how much scholarship Sam Bob, F. Nat and dad imparted on me and/or to each other, however, I can say with absolute certainty those boys gave a young lawyer a "world class education" if you know what I mean.

Sam Bob Raulston was one of the finest trial lawyers I have ever known.

Soon after I arrived in Jasper, Tenn., to start practicing law, our firm was involved in a "horrible" case. Without going into specifics, what part of the word "horrible" do you not understand?

One afternoon I went in to see Sam Bob and I told him I did not want to be personally involved in the defense of our firm's client (the case was that bad!). There was not a moment of hesitation in Sam Bob's response.

Sam Bob promptly told me that in this firm "we are lawyers." We represent the good and the bad. Sam assured me if it were not for lawyers representing evil people, then evil people would take over and anybody (especially good people) would be muzzled, trampled and subject to incarceration not to mention the theft of their property and their rights. Sam pointed out this grim reality which sadly represents the history of the world.

> *Sam assured me if it were not for lawyers representing evil people, then evil people would take over and anybody would be muzzled, trampled and subject to incarceration not to mention the theft of their property and their rights.*

Sam Bob promptly told me that if I did not have the stomach to provide a proper defense for our firm's client he would "show me the highway." Sam Bob then told me in a very kind, fatherly fashion that his father, Sam Polk Raulston, had given him the same "highway" lecture when he was a young lawyer.

I needed the lecture from Sam Bob. I went back to my office where hopefully I learned to be a "lawyer."

Although over the years, I have turned down many cases. I hope I have not been accused of turning down a case because of public sentiment or because I will become unpopular. I hope I have never been accused of failing to point out the obvious. I hope I am considered an eccentric.

<u>LIFE'S LESSON:</u>

Find a profession you love and enjoy. If you don't have the stomach to do the unpleasant, then hit the highway promptly! Do something else.

---

*Note: Sam Bob Raulston was killed in an automobile accident on July 22, 1986. Sam Bob Raulston was a great law partner. I regret never conveying my gratitude to Sam.

The Difference Between Gratitude and Getting Stabbed in the Back

*I*n one of my Life's Lessons, I mentioned my friend John Hewgley. Quoting from John's wisdom: "If you stab me once shame on you, if you stab me twice shame on me."

Let me expand on John's quote and give further comment.

Over the years, I have kept people out of jail, gotten people good jobs that altered their lives, assisted people or their children professionally, helped people get professional license, taken up for people when being criticized, and more. For these acts of kindness or courtesies, I did not expect a statue of me to be placed on the town square or have children named after me, but I certainly expected some good will or just a speck of gratitude. Certainly, I felt those whom I had extended a great favor or kindness would never stab me in the back. *Don't kid yourself!*

> *I did not expect a statue of me to be placed on the town square or have children named after me, but I certainly expected some good will or just a speck of gratitude.*

In today's world, the terms "gratitude," "loyalty" and "appreciation" are not in everyone's vocabulary. But I advise: just get over it!

For those you feel owe you some gratitude or appreciation, consider the following six points:

1. Come to grips with what you consider a big favor or courtesy. Was it really that big of a deal? Just because you have been helpful to somebody does not mean they should be eternally indebted to you nor does it mean they should remember you with fondness until their dying breath. Decide if you really did someone *that* great a favor before you have an expectation.

2. Expect nothing for simple courtesies or just doing the right thing. I repeat — expect nothing!

3. Suppose you have done somebody a life-altering favor and you expect some good will or appreciation. Suppose you need a favor returned. Suppose the person from whom you expect to "call in the favor" or the person who you consider "owes you one" comes to you

and says, for whatever reason, they can't support your endeavor or request. The person gives the reason, expresses appreciation and acknowledges gratitude for past considerations. Under these circumstances you should thank the beneficiary of your favor for their candor and reaffirm that you look forward to "doing business with them in the future." This situation represents "doing good business" in what I consider to be a very honorable fashion.

> *Lack of gratitude or loyalty, in my opinion, is a matter of character.*

4. We cannot support our best friends on every issue. Such is impossible. However, be honest and forthcoming about your position.

5. For those in this world who do not understand the word gratitude, who do not understand loyalty, who do not understand the word fidelity or who will stab an old friend in the back without reservation, this is not "business." Stabbing an old friend in the back is despicable.

6. Lack of gratitude or loyalty, in my opinion, is a matter of character.

LIFE'S LESSON:

Graciously acknowledge and release from an obligation friends who come to you and tell you they cannot support your every position or desire. More often than not, this isn't personal. People who come to you in this manner are the type of people you can and want to do business with in the future. Your relationship with these individuals will be strengthened. Without exception people appreciate being "let off the hook." You can warmly look forward to doing business with these folks down the road. Typically those in this category are more helpful in the future.

For those who do not understand the word gratitude, fidelity and/or appreciation, you should forgive them in a Biblical way and check them off your list, but never let them see your back again. I repeat never. When opportunity comes (and trust me it will) be ready to "pull the trigger" when you catch a former beneficiary of a big favor in your crosshairs. Thankless ingrates not only lack character but never liked you in the first place. If you do not pull the trigger those in this group will have less respect for you and will stab you in the back again with impunity when the opportunity arises. Revenge is best served cold.

Rotten Apple

By June Grimes
Jasper, Tenn.

*H*er shoes were taupe beige tie-ups and looked much like what a man would wear. Her skirts were khaki and her blouses were plain cotton with little feminine detail. She was thin, angular and athletic of build. She wore her gray hair very short, with a standing crest of waves at the crown. At the age that I remember her, she also had a feathering of hair on her upper lip. Any student at Richard Hardy Memorial School in the mid to late 1950s would easily recognize this description of our most dreaded and feared junior high teacher, whom I will simply refer to as "Ms. F." This teacher stands out in my mind as the embodiment of the first real life lesson I learned outside of home.

I was a happy student at RHMS for all six years before Ms. F became my teacher. We were afforded music, art, youth theatrical performances and above average educational instruction as students, which was out of the norm for many small schools. The fine art work displays and the beautiful building and grounds were enough to make a young child proud to be a part of it all. I also took personal pride in being acknowledged for good deportment. Never had I ever been paddled or sent to the principal's office. I was often chosen to be a leader of student activity groups. In the earlier grades, acknowledgement was indicated by being given class room responsibilities such as dusting the blackboards and carrying important papers to the principal's office.

But it was with great trepidation that I entered the seventh grade to face the notorious math teacher, Ms. F. I had done well enough in general math classes, but I knew I was not a star math student. Ms. F projected sternness, perfectionism and "I am smarter than you" qualities to those around her. She was famous for the math word problems that she would task her students to solve. I remember having an engineer neighbor help me arrive at the correct answer, but Ms. F did not accept his methodology. Her teaching style was direct and included sending students to the blackboard to complete math problems of her particular design. I made every effort to avoid going to the board because I wasn't sure I had the answers right and I was self-conscious about standing in front of the entire class. My discomfort increased tenfold when I attempted to complete a math problem on the board and she sarcastically called another student's name to come up to the board and correct my mistake. She did not dismiss me or tell me to return to my seat. After the giggles of the other students died down, I was left standing, not knowing whether to be seated or to enrage her by returning to my desk and risk more biting disparagement.

Being called on in class became another style of torture. I was not alone in being victimized — other students suffered similar ostracism. She would call on a student and when a correct response was not given promptly, she would make an unkind remark and move on to the next apprehensive student. My math skills hit rock bottom and my confidence in my abilities was trampled. I became a nervous, intimidated student.

The final breaking point came one spring afternoon. Ms. F called me to the office just as school ended. She handed me a workbook sheet on which I had incorrectly completed a math problem. She asked that I come into the study hall and correct it. I had never been detained after school and I was very aware that I was joining the group of detention squatters in the study hall. I settled into a desk in the front of the room distancing myself from the trouble makers and reprobates. I tried with great effort to focus on the assigned work problem. I was distracted and was aware of the other students leaving the room after completing their detention time. I turned my worksheet in at least twice for it to be returned to me by Ms. F. I began to worry that my parents would be expecting me to come home very soon. This did not seem to bother Ms. F that I was there longer than was usual. I think that my frustration and that of Ms. F came to a head when I erased a hole in the flimsy workbook paper trying to get the problem worked. Just the memory of the looks of that eraser worn paper is enough to make me wince even now.

> *A 'rotten apple' could spoil the entire barrel.*

Finally Ms. F called me forward to her desk and took out a paddle and paddled me. Though there was no permanent damage, my math "soul" was damaged for a lifetime.

Ms. F dismissed me with few words and I walked to my home crying as hard as I can ever remember doing. My mom was aghast at my swollen, tear streaked face. She listened to my disgraceful account. As my parents were given to do, they did not rant and rave about the teachers or school leadership. My parents simply consoled me and that was the end of that. It was not until many years later that I learned my mother had visited the school the following day and addressed the issue.

I did not return to my beloved Richard Hardy Elementary School the following year.

As I grew to maturity, I never regained any confidence in my math abilities. Thanks to the rotten apple experience of my seventh grade year, I felt I would need intensive therapy if I were ever to get past my fear of math after that.

LIFE'S LESSON:

The lesson I learned from this youthful experience was that a "rotten apple" could spoil the entire barrel. I have worked with groups of people for years and have seen this "rotten apple" situation happen over and over. "Bad apple behavior" can be infectious and affect the outcome of many well-intended efforts. Left unchecked, such behavior can be ruinous to institutions such as schools, businesses, families as well as individual potential.

The Constable

By Graham Swafford

I want to give a political lesson.

In 1978, I graduated from law school. I knew I had passed the bar exam when I walked out of the exam hall.

As I was taking the bar exam, Sharon was packing our worldly possessions for our trip home to Marion County, Tenn.

We arrived in Marion County two days later and I started practicing law the next day. My father and Sam Bob Raulston were waiting on me. I guess back in those days waiting on results of a bar exam was just a minor nuisance I did not need to worry about.

I don't mean to brag, but I thought I had done pretty well in law school. I had even helped a fellow write a book. However, I was about to be introduced to the "real world" that had been totally omitted in college, law school and the academic world.

> **"What the heck is a constable?"**

I had been home from law school several weeks and my mother was on the ballot running for political office. I was instructed to go to a community and hand out cards on my mother's behalf.

I have always resisted working the ballot boxes. I typically think most people have pretty much made up their minds when they arrive at the election poll. In my opinion, it makes people mad or irritates them to be harangued by election pole workers. I might be wrong and many of my readers might disagree.

My law partner, Mark Raines, tells me that I could write a how-to book on managing or running campaigns; however, he does not think I am the best "retail" politician he has ever seen, not to mention he does not think I am very good at all in electioneering. I think Mark was trying to be gentle in his opinion of my talents.

At any rate, when I arrived at the election box, everyone was extremely cordial. I had sort of psyched myself up for the occasion. I had convinced myself it was an important day. We had a congressional race, gubernatorial race, senatorial race, etc. My mother was running for superintendent of schools. It was clear to the casual observer, or at least it was clear to the successful scholar who had just graduated from law school, that we were going to be voting for folks who might have the potential to not only make a difference but change the world.

It did not cross my mind that my views would not be shared by the "average

Joe."

Within 30 seconds after my introduction and getting familiar with my fellow poll workers several things quickly became apparent:

1. Few people were impressed with my recent academic success.

2. Few people were concerned about domestic policy or what was going on at the Federal Reserve.

There was not one mention of foreign affairs, peace or tranquility, the economy, good public policy, etc., nor was there mention about keeping us out of war.

There was no discussion about abortion, taxation, gun control or the Lord's preference in the election if he even cared.

In the real world, the only thing the citizens who were voting on that particular day were concerned about was the "constable race."

The entire day all I heard about was the constable race!

I was told, in breathless tones, the qualification of one constable, in particular. Every night when he went home, this man walked to the house, and just before entering in the back door, would turn around, pull out his pistol and shoot at a hubcap on a tree, hitting it every time with pinpoint accuracy.

I do not mean to show my ignorance, but I had graduated from college, served in the military, graduated from a pretty good accredited law school, and nobody (I repeat — not even one professor or anybody) had ever mentioned the constable.

Sometime around midday the thought flashed across my mind — "What in the heck is a constable?"

By the end of the day, I was contemplating buying a pistol and seeing if I could "shoot a hubcap on a tree behind the house." I wondered how Sharon would take to shooting at hub caps. I was confident Sharon's mother would not be impressed with a son-in-law in Marion County who could hit a hub cap with a pistol.

LIFE'S LESSONS:

Especially relating to politics:

Lesson 1:

In politics you need to have an understanding of what people are thinking, what voters believe and how voters are motivated. The mood of the public doesn't necessarily make a speck of sense — Get over it!

Public opinion or the mood of the public will change on a dime. Get over it!

Those politicians who do not understand and/or read the mood of the people will do so at their own peril.

Lesson 2:

If you do not understand the "constable" or the "sheriff's" race in county politics without explanation (I repeat — without explanation) you do not need to be in politics!

Note: Only a few remaining Tennessee counties still have constables.
Typically, before the arrival of the automobile, the constable was the fellow who served process and had some limited law enforcement authority. Most counties have abolished the position of constable for a number of reasons not to mention liability, lack of control, etc. In the remaining counties that still have constables, you might see a constable driving around in a squad car (paid for in 100 percent of the cases by the constable himself) not really associated with any law enforcement agency. In my opinion constables are a thing of the past.

Express Gratitude

By Graham Swafford

*I*n August of 1965, I found myself at Camp Lookout, which was my fourth summer camp that summer.

I hated summer camp. I hated tents. I hated camp food. I hated crafts. I hated camp games. I hated singing camp songs including, but particularly, Kumbaya. I hated everything about the camping experience, not to mention bugs and public showers. I repeat — so as not to create confusion among any readers who might be confused — I hated camping!

> *I am convinced that if we had been from Iraq and my mother and Reid Wilson had been part of the Taliban I would have ended up married to all four of the Wilson girls.*

One can but speculate why I was sent to so many camps. I preferred running around unsupervised in downtown South Pittsburg, Tenn. I guess I was a precocious, energetic child.

Fortunately for me, on the first day at Camp Lookout, my path crossed with the camp administrator, Rev. Reid Wilson.

Other than my parents, my sister, my children and of course my wife, Reid Wilson was the finest person I have ever known. Reid Wilson and I connected immediately. Reid understood.

The Holston Conference of the United Methodist Church transferred Reid and his wife, Marjorie and their daughters to South Pittsburg's Holly Avenue Methodist Church in 1965 in a mid-term shuffle of ministers.

My mother loved Rev. Reid Wilson and his wife, Marjorie. Reid and Marjorie had four daughters. I am convinced that if we had been from Iraq and my mother and Reid Wilson had been part of the Taliban I would have ended up married to all four of the Wilson girls. I am not sure the girls or Marjorie Wilson would have been keen about such a marital arrangement, but my mother and Reid were not at all hesitant or queasy about a little dissatisfaction.

Reid Wilson told me, without reservation, I needed to marry Sharon.

Several years ago, Reid acquired Alzheimer's disease. I spoke at Reid's funeral which was nice, but one of the great regrets I have in life is the fact that I did not go to Johnson City when Reid was alert and express my gratitude and appreciation along with the fact that Reid and Marjorie Wilson changed my life.

LIFE'S LESSON:
As you go through life, there will be three or four people who make a difference. Do not miss the opportunity of expressing your gratitude before it is too late.

*Note: In June 2012, I flew to Johnson City and took Marjorie out to lunch. Marjorie is doing well.

Bible Combo

By Ronald Ramsey
Jasper, Tenn.

*O*ver the years, I have served five different charges in the Holston Conference in East Tennessee. At each one I have noticed one thing that is always true: so many in the church know so little about the Bible. If the Bible really is our spiritual food then I believe that many Christians are on a diet!

> *If the Bible really is our spiritual food then I believe that many Christians are on a diet!*

Think about your church. What is the average attendance for Sunday morning worship? What is the attendance at Sunday School or Bible Study? If you have a prayer service, how many people in your church come out for it?

If you are like most churches, then the attendance at any time of study is much smaller than your worship time. Many may say that this is good or at least as it should be, but that is wrong. Every Christian needs to feed themselves through Bible Study. Many of our church members are dying of starvation!

We need a Bible combo! What is a Bible combo? Like a combo meal at a restaurant, the Bible combo is made up of two forms of food and a beverage. Here is the menu:

Entrée: The meat for a Christian is the Word of God! We need to read the Word, meditate on the Word and we need to study the Word. You can flavor it to make it easier to eat, but you must eat it! We are called in the Bible itself to devour the Word and to let it settle in our stomachs. We all need the nourishment and sustenance that can only come from either drinking the milk of the Word of God for those who are young, or eating the meat of the Word of God for those who are more mature.

Side Dish: Prayer is not the lesser thing, but what completes the balanced meal. It contains everything that is not found in the entrée that is essential to life! It contains all the vitamins and minerals that are found in the vegetable portion as well as the quick energy of the potato part of the meat and potatoes meal. Prayer makes our diet balanced and enables us to build our spiritual bodies for all we have to face in these days in which we live!

Drink: We need to drink in the Spirit of God! We need to have our lives refreshed through the direct presence of God with us and in us! Our bodies are mostly water and we need water and other fluids to keep our bodies running smoothly. We also need a good dose of the Holy Spirit to make our spiritual lives run smoothly. Some may say they do not need the Holy Spirit, but how can you live a spiritual life without the Spirit?

With this balanced meal we will be stronger Christians making stronger families, making stronger churches, making stronger communities, making a better world! This is our call to change the world by being changed ourselves!

So come on! Find yourself a Bible Study you can be part of. If your church isn't offering one, ask the pastor to start one. Churches in Marion County are well-known for their good meals at special gatherings. May we also be known for our even better spiritual meals we all receive through our Bible studies! I pray that you will be hungrier for God and His Word than you are for breakfast, lunch or supper!

LIFE'S LESSON:

We need to partake in the Word of God and prayer, and drink in the Spirit of God, in order to have a balanced spiritual life.

A Change of Scenery

By Graham Swafford

*S*ince the day I got out of law school, clients have honored me with their confidence, representing them in serious criminal matters in both state and federal courts.

Without going into details, there have been occasions when I have enjoyed spectacular results with legal matters I have been entrusted to handle.

I would like to mention a disturbing fact that I have seen repeatedly over the 35 years I have practiced law. Law school never mentioned this problem.

> *Here I had done all of this great legal work and the thankless client had gotten into trouble again.*

Periodically, when I have extracted a client from a problem or gotten favorable results, the family is appreciative. I have had mothers hug me and literally weep with gratitude.

Typically under these circumstances, clients and their families say they are going to "do right" and I will "never see them again" while all along profusely wailing "Thank you, Graham!" I have even had folks suggest my arrival was divine intervention (which I sort of doubt), but in all modesty, I will take ecclesiastical credit. So, under these circumstances, I have feelings of accomplishment not to mention it is good for my ego.

When I first got out of law school and enjoyed these moments of spectacular success, I actually believed the clients and/or their families *every time* when they said "never again would they do wrong" shrieking all along they have met the Lord.

I do not mean to sound naïve, but to this day I truly believe these people and/or their families are sincere in their expressions that they "learned their lesson" and have "met the Lord" or whatever and in the future they will "do right and the American justice system will never see them again."

I had been practicing law just a short time when I got a call on a late Saturday night from a former grateful client's mother. Apparently her son, whom I had undeservedly extracted from a real indiscretion, had gotten into trouble again and was down at the jail.

The first time this happened I was surprised and shocked. Unfortunately, over the years, this scenario has repeated itself time and time again with predictable certainty.

There was a time in my life when these calls of relapse made me mad. There were times when these calls of relapse made me sad. And on a couple occasions these calls just made me sick. Here I had done all of this great legal work and the thankless client had gotten into trouble again, literally breaking the hearts of loved ones who, by the way, had paid generous attorney fees.

One day, when a particularly memorable client from an exceptional family relapsed and was arrested, I had a moment of realization.

It dawned on me that in all probability the client did not mean to get into trouble again and really wanted to "do right." After all, sitting in the county jail provides no creature comforts nor satisfies any intellectual curiosity.

The reason my client had gotten into trouble again and/or relapsed was simply the fact that they went back to their old environment with their old friends at their old haunts. There had, in reality, been no change.

However, when I have extracted individuals from problems (regardless of the type problem) and they hit the road and get a "change of scenery," the chance of a successful rehabilitation is dramatically increased.

LIFE'S LESSON:

If you are serious about making a change in your life, more often than not, you need a change of scenery. Nobody can withstand constant temptation.

The environment/friends or haunts that got you in trouble the first time will get you in trouble again — every time!

Most people think the above "Life's Lesson" does not apply to them or simply think the lesson can be ignored to which I say: "Impossible."

Note: The above lesson applies to not only criminal matters but other problems like bad school experience, bad job, bad marriage, substance problems, etc. More often than not, a change of scenery is absolutely required for successful change or recovery.

Everybody Has a Streak

By Graham Swafford

When I was a little boy attending church at Holly Avenue Methodist in South Pittsburg, Tenn., I was indoctrinated with the dangers of sin.

Early on, sin had a certain allure or attraction, if you catch my drift.

I never considered myself to be a world class expert on sin; however, I was fairly well-read, if you know what I mean. In the big scheme of things, I never thought my transgressions or sins were that bad. Heck, I could justify anything.

I have a secretary named Brandy Pruitt who has told me "sin is sin" and all sins are the same. My minister, Ron Ramsey, is a rather thoughtful fellow and he has told me pretty much the same thing, pointing out Romans 3:23 which Biblically supports the position that all of us are sinners.

> *I never thought my transgressions or sins were that bad. Heck, I could justify anything.*

Practicing law for 35 years, I have seen untold evil that would curl your hair. I have seen situations where I was convinced the devil would win. I am convinced there is a devil who is *real and on the job* and has each of my readers in his sights. I know the devil personally wants Graham Swafford.

I am of the opinion (but not totally certain) that all sins are *not* the same. In the sweet by and by I hope that some sins will not be treated as harshly as others. I am of the opinion the really serious sins involve the corruption of children and families. I might be wrong but the above represents my opinion. There are some sins that, hopefully in the sweet by and by, I can get away with or talk my way around.

With the above background, let me give you a universal observation. I am of the opinion that *everybody has something.* I had a client come into my office one day and tell me with great authority that everybody in the world (everybody apparently includes all my readers) has a "streak of road tramp and a streak of larceny" in them. I am inclined to agree with my client's observation.

LIFE'S LESSONS:

There is a devil! The devil is real and he is after you.

Everyone has a streak of road tramp and/or a streak of larceny in them. The only difference is some people can control or conceal their urges and some people have been forgiven. Everybody means everybody!

Why Judges Should Not Ask Questions

By Judge Buddy D. Perry
Winchester, Tenn.

Good lawyers know not to ask questions of a witness unless the lawyer knows the answer. Surprise answers seldom help win lawsuits. A corollary to this rule is that judges should not ask witnesses questions. Judges appear much smarter if they let the lawyers do the work.

I failed to follow the rule and I suffered the consequences.

I am a circuit judge, which in Tennessee means that I travel several rural counties, along with three colleagues, and we try mostly civil and criminal jury trials. The days that all judges dread are the civil non-jury days when we have to hear divorces, child custody issues, and the occasional general sessions appeal. It was during a sessions appeal case that I violated the rule.

My home is in Franklin County. Our county is a prosperous community on the southwestern edge of the Appalachian Mountains. Our Judicial District includes the mountain community of Grundy County, three counties in an area generally referred to as the Sequatchie Valley, and on the northeastern edge of the District is Rhea County, home to the famous Scope's Monkey Trial. We try cases in the same courthouse used by Clarence Darrow and William Jennings Bryan.

On the day that I will never forget, I was holding court in Bledsoe County. The courtroom should have been torn down 20 years ago. Instead, the County Fathers unsuccessfully tried to remodel an outdated facility. My only reason for sharing this information is to tell the readers that it is impossible to hear in the courtroom, and it is not unusual to ask a witness or a lawyer to repeat their answer or argument.

I asked the clerk to call the first case, and he called *Smith v. Smith*. I thought the case was a session appeal matter, but I was wrong.

I had briefly reviewed the file before court, and I had some information about the case. Mr. Smith had, without the benefit of counsel, sued his ex-wife for the return of some of his personal property. The ex-wife was represented by a very capable, young, Pikeville lawyer.

Mr. Smith had either been working on the farm or he planned to leave court and go to the farm. Under his faded overalls was a sleeveless, white t-shirt. His size 13 boots supported his 270 pound frame. The ex-wife was dressed for court and appeared none too happy about the process.

Since the lady was represented by counsel, I started by asking the young lawyer why the case was in circuit court and not in general sessions court.

He responded, "Judge, the local judge was not going to be available for several days, and the clerk and I agreed that this was a case that needed attention, and we thought you would agree to go ahead and hear the case for us."

The young attorney's answer and his quiet smile should have given me warning. On this particular occasion, I failed to perceive the unusual nature of the case.

"Aw man, you don't know what a shot of leg is!"

Without sensing the direction the case was about to turn, I arrogantly jumped in and asked Mr. Smith the first of a series of stupid questions. I started, "Mr. Smith, why are you here?"

"To have my case heard, Judge." Fair enough I thought; should have not asked that question.

"I mean, Mr. Smith, what relief do you want from the court?"

"I want my stuff, Judge."

"You're what, Mr. Smith? I did not hear you."

In a loud and almost angry voice, he said, "I just want my stuff, Judge."

I continued my questioning, "What stuff?"

"My tools, my clothes, and my fishing boat."

Thinking that I could quickly end the matter, I asked the ex-wife if she was willing to give her ex-husband his "stuff."

She responded, "I have told him over and over that he can have his stuff. I do not understand why we are here."

Thinking how smart I am that I had resolved the problem with just a few questions, I said, "Mr. Smith, I think we have resolved the problem." I was wrong!

"Judge," he said, "She always says that, but every time I go to get my stuff, I end up getting a shot of leg and not my stuff."

"What did you say?" I asked.

He repeated his answer, "Every time I go to get my stuff, I end up getting a shot of leg and not my stuff."

On this day, I had a large civil non-jury docket, and the courtroom was packed with litigants and lawyers. The Chattanooga lawyers seemed particularly interested in my sessions court case. I now suspect that the young lawyer and the clerk had alerted the members of the bar to pay attention to this case.

I asked the fatal, stupid question, "What is a shot of leg?"

Without any hesitation Mr. Smith answered, "Aw man, you don't know what a shot of leg is!" The courtroom exploded with laughter. Everyone but me knew, and it finally occurred to me what he was talking about.*

Trying to appear dignified — I am a judge — the solution to the problem occurred to me.

"Mr. Smith," I said, "I am from Franklin County, and that is 75 miles away, and you need the help of a local judge. It is clear to me that we should have never received this from the general session judge, and I am going to send this case back to him to be heard."

"Mr. Smith, I have no doubt that he will give you the proper assistance; maybe even go with you to help you get your stuff."

On this particular day in rural Bledsoe County Courtroom, I learned a simple life's lesson.

LIFE'S LESSON:

*If a judge wants to appear dignified and knowledgeable,
then the judge best not ask any questions.*

*Note: For those readers who do not understand Bledsoe County vernacular, think sex.

I Missed My Big Chance

By Graham Swafford

MATTHEW 25

³⁴*Then the King will say to those on his right 'Come, you who are blessed by my Father; take your inheritance, the kingdom prepared for you since the creation of the world.'*

³⁵*For I was hungry and you gave me something to eat, I was thirsty and you gave me something to drink, I was a stranger and you invited me in,*

³⁶*I needed clothes and you clothed me, I was sick and you looked after me, I was in prison and you came to visit me.*

³⁷*Then the righteous will answer him, Lord, when did we see you hungry and feed you, thirsty and give you something to drink?*

³⁸*When did we see you a stranger and invite you in or needing clothes and clothe you?*

³⁹*When did we see you sick or in prison and go visit you?*

⁴⁰*The king will reply "I tell you the truth, whatever you did for one of the least of these brothers of mine you did for me."*

⁴¹*Then he will say to those on his left, "Depart from me, you who have cursed, into the eternal fire prepared for the devil and his angels.*

⁴²*For I was hungry and you gave me nothing to drink.*

⁴³*I was a stranger and you did not invite me in. I needed clothes and you did not clothe me, I was sick and in prison and you did not look after me."*

⁴⁴*They also will answer, "Lord when did we see you hungry or thirsty or a stranger or needing clothes or sick or in prison, and did not help you?"*

⁴⁵*He will reply, "I tell you the truth, whatever you did not do for one of the least of these, you did not do for me."*

⁴⁶*Then they will go away to eternal punishment, but the righteous to eternal life.*

So here are the facts.

Over the years, Sharon and I have traveled places.

Wherever we find ourselves, those pan-handling for money penetrate through the crowd and come straight to me asking for a dollar. The request is usually accompanied with a sad story.

Sharon has repeatedly pointed out that some people "can spot a sucker a mile away." I guess Sharon thinks I am a sucker (you can draw your own conclusions on that statement).

Sharon has repeatedly pointed out that some people 'can spot a sucker a mile away.'

Several years ago, we found ourselves in front of Union Station in Washington, D.C. Union Station is probably one of the most distinctive, if not most beautiful, buildings in the world.

As I was leaving the building, a beggar approached me asking for some money. I don't know what made this individual different from hundreds of others who have approached me over the years — there was a look in his eye, an expression on his face and a tone in his voice that haunts me to this day.

For some unknown reason I blew the gentleman off and curtly ignored his request. I cannot forget the look on the fellow's face or the pain in his eye.

Looking back, I wish I had given the gentleman a couple of dollars. I am not naïve. The man probably would have bought some drugs or some beer. Sharon will confirm I have wasted money before.

Yet, to this day I have wondered if this was my big chance.

LIFE'S LESSON:

"I tell you the truth, whatever you did for one of the least of these brothers of mine, you did for me."

I still remain haunted over this particular gentleman.

Marital Advice

By Graham Swafford

*G*iving newlyweds marital advice is nothing new. In August of 1975, I drove to Memphis where Sharon Carson and I were married two weeks before I started law school.

Without exception, when the mother-in-law and the wife's sister turn against a man, he 'does not have a prayer.'

Marital advice was freely given in South Pittsburg, Tenn., prior to my departure. Needless to say, I got a lot of advice — most of which absolutely blew over my head.

I was given all the standard stuff: "tell her you love her every night" or "don't go to bed mad" or "try to take a trip ever summer," etc.

Before I left for Memphis to get married, my father gave me some advice that I thought was absolutely crucial and made a real difference. The rest of the advice was generally worthless.

The advice from my dad was simple and to the point:

"Capture the mother-in-law and your wife's sister. If you capture the mother-in-law and your new wife's sister, you can get away with anything three or four times. On the other hand, if the mother-in-law and the sister-in-law get mad at you, they will ultimately "get you" regardless of the facts and regardless of how fine a fellow you are."

I have practiced law 35 years. I have represented folks in literally hundreds of divorces. Without exception, when the mother-in-law and the wife's sister turn against a man, he "does not have a prayer."

Pat Carson and Patty Carson Bowlin were not hard to capture. I hope I have lived up to their expectations.

LIFE'S LESSON:

For young grooms: Capture your wife's mother and the new sister-in-law. If you capture the mother-in-law and the sister-in-law you can get away with absolutely any type of nonsense (no matter how egregious) three or four times, if not more. On the other hand, when you lose the mother-in-law and the sister-in-law, it is just a matter of time before they get you!

Experiences of a Naval Aviator

By Howard G. Swafford Sr.
Jasper, Tenn.

To understand my joys and sorrows as a Naval Aviator, it might be advisable to describe my young years prior to enlisting in the Navy.

I was born in Jasper, Tenn., and lived principally in South Pittsburg, Tenn. My father was a barber and a policeman. He would lose his job and there were hard times. I carried and sold newspapers. I milked a cow every morning. I graduated from South Pittsburg High School in May 1936 and entered the University of Tennessee in September 1936 at the age of 16. I hitch-hiked to and from Knoxville. I had saved $75 gardening for Mrs. C. R. Kellerman and that is the only money I had to go to the university. That money paid for my books and tuition and I fired furnaces for my room and waited on tables for my food. The university had a help program that paid $15 per month — the job came to me with the help of J. Leonard Raulston who worked for the university at that time.

During the summer, I sold Bibles and graduated from U.T. in 1941. Other than attending classes and working, I went out for wrestling for which I acquired a letter and was captain of the team.

World War II began on December 7, 1941, and I volunteered for the Navy in April 1942. My first duty was to take flying lessons at Lovell Field in Chattanooga, Tenn., and Carl Gibson was my instructor. My pre-flight training was at the University of Georgia and Intermediate was at Lambert Field in St. Louis, Mo., after which I was sent to Pensacola, Fla., for final training. You can never imagine how proud I was to be a cadet at Pensacola and to win the wings and a commission in February 1944.

The Navy gave me advanced training for three months at Jacksonville, Fla., and after a vacation, ordered me to San Diego where I waited around a couple of months and was then placed on a Baby Carrier and sent to Guadalcanal.

My specialty was flying an OS2U airplane off of a battleship. My job was to spot or direct the cannon where to shoot.

In Guadalcanal, I looked around where the Marines had fought the previous years then one day they flew me to Hawaii where I was placed on the battleship, South Dakota, in September 1944 as a pilot on the observation plane OS2U.

We headed to the Southwest Pacific for the Philippine campaign which was getting underway. The South Dakota was part of Task Force No. 3 consisting of two Essex type aircraft carriers: the battleship was to protect the carriers in the event a surface ship was able to penetrate the Task Force, which was surrounded by 14 destroyers.

No sooner had we arrived in the Southwest Pacific than Japanese aircrafts came on the scene. In late September, so many were sent against us that some penetrated the ring of vessels in the circle and I looked and one was coming straight at us! It was shot down before getting to the South Dakota.

The next day, they came again and one flew into an Essex type aircraft carrier on which Lt. Commander Robert Goodgame of South Pittsburg served and he was killed in the attack.

When we were sent out, we were to protect the Task Force. Carriers would come and go. We were 60 days at sea before seeing land. At that time it was an atoll which was coral reefs coming to the surface of the ocean and making a harbor about 10 miles wide.

The most thrilling moment of my career was at Utlithi Atoll in December 1944. One morning, early, I went to the upper deck and I looked at the armada of ships at anchor. There were five Essex type aircraft carriers; three battleships; three cruisers and 30 destroyers. I was so thrilled to be a part of such a grand armada.

During the Philippine campaign, a companion aircraft and I were assigned to pick up a pilot who had been shot down for which I was awarded an air medal.

We assisted in the capture of Saipan and Iwo Jima.

We next went to Okinawa. I was the first director of bombardment on the coast of Okinawa. The South Dakota had a nine-16-inch cannon and it was my duty to radio back and tell the director of the cannon where to shoot and after the shot, how to change the direction, if any.

After the capture of Okinawa, the Task Force then began the attack on the mainland of Japan. The British had ships in the area. Since I was a specialist in directing the cannon, I was placed on a dive bomber to give the gunners, of the British Heavy Cruiser Chesterton, directions. The reason I was placed on this dive bomber was because an OS2U was so slow it would be shot down immediately.

I directed the cannon on the British Heavy Cruiser Chesterton against the heavy industry of the Japanese City of Osaka.

In the Spring of 1945, the Battleship South Dakota went to Saipan for repairs. B-29 bombers were flying from their island to Tokyo to bomb it. Lt. Oran Kenna Woodfin, of South Pittsburg, was the pilot of a B-29 and I visited him. Later, Kenna's brother was a pilot of the first class of jet fighters.

It was about this time that the Heavy Cruiser USS Indianapolis left Saipan unescorted to go to Manila. Aulton Phillips, of Jasper, Tenn., was on their cruiser when it went down and he was out.

Shortly after this, we received word that the Atomic Bomb had been dropped and the war was over.

The South Dakota proceeded to the harbor in Japan where the treaty was signed. I was on the South Dakota which was alongside of the Battleship Missouri where the peace treaty was signed.

We then went back to San Francisco where the city gave us a party! This was a tremendous affair given by a grateful city for their returning sailors.

LIFE'S LESSON:

If I have had any success in my life, it was because of my steadfast mother, the First Baptist Church at South Pittsburg, the ambition of my father and my marriage to a noble lady of great character — Claude Galbreath of Greenville, Tenn. It is that simple.

Penny White and the 'Stampede'

By Graham Swafford

I will give you a giant lesson along with a statewide legal story. This lesson has universal application (i.e. politics, business, personal life, etc.).

On a weekly basis, the Tennessee Appellate Courts issue what is commonly referred to as the "advance sheets." In layman's terms the "advance sheets" represent cases decided and opinions rendered by both the Tennessee Court of Appeals and the Tennessee Supreme Court. I read the advance sheets every week. When I was a little boy, I remember my father reading the advance sheets.

> *I have never been considered for the Tennessee Supreme Court, however, hope springs eternal.*

As we all know, all judges on the Tennessee Supreme Court and the Tennessee Court of Appeals (these are the folks that write the decisions in the advance sheets) are great scholars and excellent craftsmen of the English language. All opinions written by the Tennessee Appellate Courts are always lucid, clear, insightful, entertaining not to mention inspiring and never wrong. I *applaud* the brilliant decisions I read every week in the Tennessee Advance Sheets with unrestrained support not to mention admiring enthusiasm.

On the other hand, for attorneys who have been to the rodeo a few years, it becomes quickly apparent that there are some appellate judges who might be entitled to a little more applause than others, if you know what I mean.

In this "Life's Lesson" I want to tell a story that hopefully conveys a lesson sooner if not later to be faced by everyone. I must admit I have a personal weakness in this area.

I want to tell you the story of Penny White.

In 1990, Penny White was circuit judge in upper East Tennessee, a secure position she could have probably enjoyed with distinction and great personal satisfaction until the end of time, if she so desired. Being a circuit judge in Tennessee is a pretty big deal.

In 1992, Judge White was appointed to the Tennessee Court of Appeals. Being on the Tennessee Court of Appeals in Tennessee is a really big deal.

In 1994, lightning struck. Penny White received a telephone call from the governor's office and she had just been appointed to the Tennessee Supreme

Court.

Being a justice on the Tennessee Supreme Court is *giant*. Candidly, I have never been considered for the Tennessee Supreme Court, however, hope springs eternal. If any of my readers run across the governor and run out of conversation you might want to mention that Graham Swafford in Jasper, Tenn., is available to serve on the Tennessee Supreme Court and he can be in Nashville to accept the responsibility "at moment's notice."

I personally do not know Penny White, other than perhaps the minimal contact lawyers across the state typically enjoy with each other. My sister, Claudia, tells me that she is a close personal friend of Penny White and Penny White is a fine person. I point out (for those who do not already know) my sister, Claudia, and her husband, Bill, seem to know and enjoy a confidential relationship with everyone on the planet.

I thought Penny White could write the best appellate decisions of any judge I have ever read. I remember reading one of her decisions in the advance sheets and the decision was so well-crafted I became personally saddened realizing my inadequacies and the fact that such ability and/or talent was "just not in me."

In 1996, the case of *State of Tennessee v. Richard Odom a/k/a Otis Smith* arrived at the Tennessee Supreme Court for review and decision. By this time Penny White was a relatively new justice on the Tennessee Supreme Court which consisted of five justices. Simply stated, Justice White was a late arriver — one of the five but certainly not the leader of the pack.

The defendant, Richard Odom a/k/a Otis Smith, was a gold-plated, world class, piece of work. Notwithstanding the fact that Odom a/k/a Smith had been involved in a homicide in Mississippi, the court record revealed that in 1992 while in Memphis, Tenn., he broke into an old lady's house, beat her up, robbed her, raped her and finally, if all that was not enough, concluded a busy day by brutally killing the poor woman.

Odom a/k/a Smith was charged with murder and the State of Tennessee sought the death penalty.

In lawyer talk, Odom a/k/a Smith "was factually a horrible case." This was *not* one of those cases where attorneys could use the standard excuses (i.e. "self defense" or the victim "deserved it," or "it was not my fault" or you got the "wrong dude," or "I am being picked on by the police," or "life isn't fair" or "it was my parent's fault" or "I'm sexually repressed," etc.).

The murder case was tried before the Circuit Court of Shelby County, Tenn., and not only was Richard Odom a/k/a Otis Smith convicted of first degree murder, but he was given the death penalty. I am typically not very supportive of the death penalty, but this case was so horrible not only would I have given Richard

I remember reading one of her decisions in the advance sheets and the decision was so well-crafted I became personally saddened realizing my inadequacies and the fact that such ability and talent was 'just not in me.'

Odom a/k/a Otis Smith the death penalty had I been on the jury, but I would have criticized the arresting officers for not "shooting the thug on the spot." The case was that clear. The case was that horrible.

Let me bring further clarity if my readers are still confused — I want no confusion. Richard Odom a/k/a Otis Smith did not enjoy the sympathy vote. Odom a/k/a Smith was a crazy, dangerous man. I am of the opinion without a shadow of doubt Odom a/k/a Smith would kill again, if released.

The decision of the jury to convict Odom a/k/a Smith of first degree murder was correct and sustained. There was a *giant legal problem*. The problem was the jury charge concerning the death penalty (which was relied upon by the jury in sentencing Odom a/k/a Smith to the death penalty which, in my opinion, he so obviously deserved) was incorrect and represented a misstatement of the law. Simply stated, the issue before the Tennessee Supreme Court was "you cannot give a defendant the death penalty on a flawed and/or incorrect jury instruction and/or a flawed statement of the law."

I thought the law was so clear it did not require a legal education to understand the fundamental legal principal that the law requires a correct application of the law in any case, not to mention a case sentencing a man to death.

The Tennessee Supreme Court sustained the underlying first degree murder conviction. I repeat the conviction of first degree murder *was not reversed*. Odom a/k/a Smith was *not released* from jail. The death sentence portion of the trial however was reversed and the case was remanded back to the Circuit Court of Shelby County, Tenn., for correction or resentencing.

I agreed with the Tennessee Supreme Court completely. It is not proper to sentence someone to die (or anything else for that matter) on a flawed jury instruction and/or an incorrect statement of the law.

I can state with absolute certainty that had the Tennessee Supreme Court not had the courage to do exactly what they did, the U.S. District Court would have reversed the sentence based on incorrect jury charge "in a heartbeat."

Penny White was not the lead justice in the case. Penny White did not write the decision reversing the death penalty with remand back Shelby County Circuit Court for correction. Penny White just concurred with an obviously correct decision. Penny White really did not have that much to do with the decision other than approving with the majority of the justices the obvious.

My guess is this case was one of hundreds reviewed by the Tennessee Supreme Court on a yearly basis and but for the dramatic consequences (or the horrible facts) the case would have been long forgotten by the justices on the Tennessee Supreme Court who heard the case in 1996. I repeat I thought it was a pretty simple issue, notwithstanding the horrible facts.

Judges need to be able to follow the law regardless of popularity. Judges should not be threatened or intimidated when they follow the law.

At the next election, when Justice White stood for election, she was targeted by victims' rights advocates, the conservative union, death penalty proponents, wack-o's and everybody else who had an axe to grind or was generally mad at the world.

Those against Justice White flooded the state with materials urging her defeat. As a result of the publicity, Penny White lost her seat on the Tennessee Supreme Court. Only 19 percent of the state's voters even voted in the election.

In my opinion, Penny White was run over by the "stampeding herd." I have no way of knowing, however I would guess Penny White "never saw it coming." Penny White was not a wild-eyed radical.

I was saddened by the defeat of Penny White. Judges need to be able to follow the law regardless of popularity. Judges should not be threatened or intimidated when they follow the law.

People are usually not very interested in a competent, unbiased judiciary until their lives or the lives of their children or their personal fortunes are at serious risk — then remarkably people want an independent, fearless judiciary that understands and can apply the common law and can then write a lucid opinion.

If I am ever elected governor of the state of Tennessee, the first thing I will do is unapologetically appoint some of my old buddies to the Tennessee Supreme Court and the Court of Appeals. The next thing I will do is appoint Penny White to the Supreme Court to make sure my buddies are supervised and craft superior opinions not to mention follow well-established law.

In my opinion the citizens of the state of Tennessee and the legal community did Penny White an injustice. Bill Frist, Don Sundquist and particularly Fred Thompson should be ashamed of themselves — they knew better.

LIFE'S LESSON:
In the game of life, you need to recognize when a stampede is headed in your direction and if you cannot control the direction of the stampede at least get your happy posterior out of the way!

The Difference Between Crazy and Genius

By Graham Swafford

ypically, as we go through life, we have the pleasure, or displeasure, however you look at it, of meeting very few geniuses.

I met no geniuses at the University of Tennessee or the Army.

I met no geniuses at the University of Tennessee or the Army.

Law school was my first experience of a place where everybody was bright and way above average smart. There were several geniuses at the University of Memphis Law School.

When I was growing up, and going to high school in South Pittsburg, there were four geniuses (maybe five) in school with me. I will not mention any names.

LIFE'S LESSON:

Most people in this world will never meet a genius. In my experience, there is a thin line between genius and crazy. There are one or two defining moments that make a difference.

Being Comfortable With Making the Ask

By H. Graham Swafford III
Nashville, Tenn.

I recently had the opportunity to hear Bill Courtenay speak on the traits of successful leaders. Bill is the founder of Classic American Hardwoods in Memphis. In 2004, he volunteered at Manassas High School coaching underprivileged student-athletes. In a period of five years, the team went from a long standing losing tradition to championship contenders. Bill and his team were the focus of the 2011 Oscar award-winning film "Undefeated."

Bill was speaking, in particular, on one of the common denominators he noticed great leaders possess. He called it "being comfortable with making the ask." At this point there were a lot of puzzled looks from within the crowd. Bill then exited the stage and went into the crowd of several hundred people. He approached a total stranger and with all eyes in the room focused intently, asked for the man's wallet. I was astonished that the stranger complied and gave Bill his wallet! The point, according to Bill, was this: To get what you really want you must be comfortable in simply asking. It is amazing what you might get in return. Now, this fellow could just as easily have asked Bill to go fly a kite. As it turned out there was a lot of cash in his wallet! This pearl of wisdom really got me thinking as I reflected on some of the "asks" over my lifetime.

> *To get what you really want you must be comfortable in simply asking. It is amazing what you might get in return.*

I have had some good "asks" over my life. By the same token, I have had some really go south. Some of the more memorable "asks" involve the solicitation of insurance to potential clients, which is what I do for a living. There was the guy who called the police upon my arrival to talk insurance. Then there was the lady who kept a pit bull leashed at her desk. I'm not making this up. When I showed up and she learned the reason for my visit she unhooked this rabid beast and away for the door I ran!

Then there was the time I met the guy who invented a device that prevents leaves and debris from getting into your home gutter. All the "gunk" just blows right off your roof instead of clogging the gutters. A real "why didn't I think of that?" moment. As it turns out, you can in fact achieve fame, fortune and glory by having your mind in the gutter. As we were talking, a commonality came up that we are both aviation enthusiasts. As he mentioned offhand that he owned an airplane, our conversation ended abruptly. I guess other folks wanted to talk to this tycoon who made his fortune with a simple, ingenious invention. On the way out, I had noticed his automobile and decided "what the heck." I wrote a note and asked if I could go flying with him and included my contact info. I placed the note on his car. As it turns out this king of the gutter was a huge University of Tennessee booster and had donated his aircraft to fly the UT coaches to all the SEC road games that season. He called me the next day and asked if I would like to fly as co-pilot. It was great fun as the chief pilot and I enjoyed all the benefits of transporting the coaches around the Southeastern Conference, including great seats, limo service to the stadium, etc.

LIFE'S LESSON

This brings me to the Life's Lesson. Even at the worst, you have to be comfortable in making the "ask." The worst thing that has happened included an angry pitbull chasing me to the door. While it wasn't very funny at the time, I look back and realize people actually keep animals at work leashed to their desk. On the other end of the spectrum, the best thing in my life came from making the "ask" when I asked my future wife out on a date. I was completely out of my league when she actually said "yes." It is amazing what can come if you just ask.

The Real Education

By Graham Swafford

My sister and I, by all accounts, enjoyed a pretty fair formal education. The walls of our offices are considered, by some, fairly impressive.

But the real education that made the difference came around the dinner table.

> *The real education that made the difference came around the dinner table.*

So here are some life lessons acquired around the dinner table:

1. If you get whipped at school, you get whipped at home. Don't confuse us with the facts and we understand it wasn't your fault.

2. We learned about "loyalty" and getting "stabbed" in the back. We learned the difference between these terms. We learned loyalty is a matter of character.

3. We learned there is a difference between "class" and "trash."

4. We learned the definition of "gratitude."

5. We learned the importance of a good dog.

6. We learned it is better for children to have an opinion and be wrong, than have no opinion at all.

7. We learned jury verdicts and elections send messages.

8. We learned to keep a secret. We learned there are some confidences you take to the grave — never to be repeated. We learned good friends know how to take secrets to the grave — once again this is a matter of character.

9. We learned a good plan well-funded beats genius every time.

10. We learned hell hath no fury like a reformed (not to mention mad) sinner.

11. We learned at the end of the day the only thing that matters is where you spend eternity and what your family thinks of you — nothing else!

12. We learned Proverbs 24:6

13. We learned Ecclesiastes 3:1-8

14. We learned the 23rd Psalm.

15. We learned the importance of reading books.

16. We learned to appreciate those who dug wells from which we benefit.

17. We learned a little gall will take you a long way.

18. We learned details are the hobgoblins of little minds.

19. We learned to identify the throne.

20. We learned it is easier to get forgiveness than permission.

21. We learned about picking the hill you want to die on (Note: Claudia was the only one who understands how to apply this lesson with any success — but we got the lesson).

22. We learned that old age, experience and treachery beats youth and enthusiasm every time.

23. We learned Matthew 6:21.

24. We learned Matthew 6:24.

25. We learned Ruth 1:16-17.

26. We learned "There but for the grace of God go I."

27. We learned what goes around comes around.

28. We learned he who bites will be bitten.

29. We learned every dog has their day.

My sister and I received a world class education.

LIFE'S LESSON:

Unforgettable life lessons learned early on around the dinner table and carried to this day, will be passed to the next generation.

The Adventures of a Wannabe Wasp
or
The Experience of a Teenaged Tennessee Girl During WWII

By Geneva Swafford Pomeroy
Glendale, OH

efore December 7, 1941, I had never heard of Pearl Harbor. It did not take me long to understand why my Aunt Eunice was so upset that Sunday afternoon when news came over the radio, about 2 pm, that the Japanese had bombed Pearl Harbor. She and Uncle Alec had four sons. The draft had begun the year before. The next day from the capitol, President Franklin D. Roosevelt made his famous "date which will live in infamy" speech. The United States was officially at war! Everyone in the United States would be involved. Hardly a soul disagreed. I would not have wanted to be a "Jap" in America at that time!

The United States was coming out of the Great Depression — the South more slowly than the rest of the nation. The production of war materials began immediately. For civilians, there was rationing of sugar, meat, gasoline, shoes, nylon, and rubber. Some women began to work in defense plants. Remember "Rosie, the riveter?" Others volunteered with such needs as rolling bandages, helping the Red Cross by knitting sweaters & socks, and volunteering in hospitals.

In spite of the sudden seriousness in our lives, there was an air of excitement, along with the sadness, as young boys went off to see the world. We teenage girls were excited when a convoy of Army vehicles drove through town and soldiers would throw out their addresses to us in hopes that we would write to them. It was big news when local Army pilot Jimmy Fitzgerald was in the area and buzzed around our little town in a PSI Fighter Plane. He would let one of his brothers or sisters know ahead of time when he would be coming. Many years later, he became a test pilot and was the second pilot, after Chuck Yeager, to break the sound barrier. He eventually had a tragic fatal crash.

My world centered around a little town 33 miles west of Chattanooga and 2 miles from the Alabama border. It is on the Tennessee River with mountains on the opposite side. You all probably have never had a reason to hear of South Pittsburg, population about 3500, unless you own a Lodge cast iron skillet, cornstick pan, or one of their Dutch-ovens. As an aside, about 10 years ago, their Dutch-oven made the front page of the Wall Street Journal when a Japanese named Hitoshi Kikuchi discovered the Lodge Dutch-oven when he signed up for two weeks' work camp in Nevada. A camp cook named "Blacktop" introduced him to the Dutch-oven and it changed his life. When he went back to Japan, he dashed off a six-page letter to the company whose name was embossed on the lid: Lodge Manufacturing Co., South Pittsburg, Tenn. His company, Buckaroo Design Inc., became the representative for the Lodge Dutch-oven, one of America's last family-owned Dutch-oven makers. After a 1997 trip to Idaho, in a travelogue, he wrote "mountain men from the Rockies tend to use Crisco, while cowboys of the Nevada desert use lard". This past weekend, the 13th "National Cornbread Festival", sponsored by Lodge Mfg. Co. and Martha White, was held in South Pittsburg. Thousands of people from near and far come to these Festivals, and the profits from them have made it a tourist town.

You all probably have never had a reason to hear of South Pittsburg, population about 3500, unless you own a Lodge cast iron skillet, cornstick pan, or one of their Dutch-ovens.

I would be remiss not to mention segregation. It didn't seem fair to me, but it was just something that was. We were taught to say "Negro" and never the other "n" word. Negroes and whites were friendly with each other, and there was only one Jewish family in our town. I wasn't aware of much talk about there being separate schools, water fountains, and public bathrooms. Negroes sat in the balcony at movies and rode in the back of the bus. They must have hated it! One of the best doctors in town was a Negro and my Daddy went to him.

As the war raged on, most of us teenage girls went on with our lives. Soon after my 17th birthday, my friend Dava Jean Martin and I were sitting in her Daddy's drugstore talking about our futures. We had just graduated from high school. Dava Jean was complaining because her parents were insisting that she go on to college. I was wishing that I could, but, to use a term which I hear being used lately, "we were of humble beginnings." There were, and still are, six of us kids. Neither of our parents finished high school, which was not uncommon at that time and place. But, what they lacked in "book learning," they made up for with good ol' common sense — especially our Mama, a gentle woman. They taught us honesty, how to work, to treat others the way that we would like to be treated, and innovation, meaning to change or make do with what we had. They saw to it that we went to school every day unless we had a fever, or measles, or chicken pox, or mumps, or the pink eye. What we did on Sunday mornings was go to Sunday School and church and that evening, youth group. There were no TVs, cell phones, blackberries, or iPod to distract us, but I distinctly remember being glued to the radio every Saturday night to hear the Hit Parade! We had lots of cousins as playmates. Actually, we had some freedoms that children do not enjoy today. Daddy just told us that if we got punished at school, we would get it again when we got home. We six kids were a bit like birds. We were cared for until we finished high school. Then, as we were able to leave the nest, one by one we flew off on our own.

Well, Dava Jean went off to college and I looked into becoming a WASP — Women Airforce Service Pilot. My duty would be to ferry new aircraft to Army air bases. But that was not to be. I wasn't old enough and some flying time was required in order to join. So, to Chattanooga I went to room with my sister and find a job. Rosa Lee, who was valedictorian of her high school class, was working for TVA and saving money to return to college. Since some of you know her, I'll tell you something that you most likely don't know about her. After she graduated from the University of Tennessee, she went to Washington DC as an intern, but *she* stayed out of trouble! Later on, she had a career as an economist with the Labor Department. As for me, because of a friend's recommendation, I got a job with Western Union, training to be a teletype operator. I was thrilled! As I recall, it paid about $14 a week, but a dollar went a long way as compared with today. One of the patriotic things to do was to entertain the soldiers at the USO. Rosa Lee and I really enjoyed their dances. This was the era of Big Band music. She met a special guy at the USO. I remember the sad day that she received a message from Bill's mother that he had been killed in action. All during the war, there was the dread of hearing that someone we knew was missing in action, wounded, or killed.

At the time, I thought of it as just an interesting job, but in retrospect, I realized that sending telegrams was very important, especially during a war.

After I learned to send and receive telegrams, I started working at Camp Forest, near Tullahoma. The pay was better, and I could save for my flying lessons. At the time, I thought of it as just an interesting job, but in retrospect, I realized that sending telegrams was very important, especially during a war. I continued patriotically enjoying dancing with the soldiers!

After working and saving for a year and a half, I resigned my job and went home to tell my parents that I was going to take flying lessons at Embry Riddle Flying School in Florida. I had to have their signature for permission. My Daddy was very upset and strongly objected. I did not want to go against his wishes, and I began to question my reasons for wanting to become a WASP. Perhaps it was because my oldest brother, Howard, was a Navy pilot. After much thought and tears, I requested and received my deposit from Embry Riddle. Little did I know that I would have another opportunity to fly!

I would like to tell you, in as few words as possible, about my brother Howard, because he set the pace for his four sisters and little brother. He, nor we, realized it at the time. In 1936, with $75 earned from doing yard work, he hitch-hiked to Knoxville and enrolled at the University of Tennessee. When our nation entered the war, he joined the Navy. After he was discharged, he came back to UT to finish undergraduate courses and go on to law school on the GI Bill. After graduation, he married one of the three females in the law college, returned to South Pittsburg, and joined the law firm of Judge John T. Raulston, who was the judge in the famous Scopes trial, also known as the "Monkey Trial." Later on, he was elected a Tennessee State Representative. He and his wife have helped many young people get a college education. Next month his granddaughter will graduate from Tennessee Law School — making her the third generation to do so. Howard, soon to be 90 years old, walks almost two miles each morning and goes to his office a part of each day.

> *Can you imagine today having eight girls sharing one bathroom?*

Having decided not to take flying lessons, I packed my bag, caught the bus to Knoxville, and enrolled at the University of Tennessee. UT had a very strong College of Home Economics with several majors within the college. I decided to major in child development, mainly because it required only one year of chemistry. I also loved children. The college has since been named the College of Education and Human Services. Some of the dorms were being used by cadets, so we girls had to double up in our dorm rooms. A suite of two rooms with a bath in between had four girls in each room. Can you imagine today having eight girls sharing one bathroom? There must have been one down the hall, but I don't remember it. Each girl had a desk and there were two sets of bunk beds in each room. My bunk mate was "Sham", who continues to be one of my best friends. We had a house mother, and no boys were allowed above the first floor. It wasn't necessary to lock our rooms unless we wanted to keep a certain girl from borrowing our clothes! We could go down the hall or to another room in as few clothes as we wished. There were check-in times and we had to have a note from home to be away from the dorm overnight.

I never took chemistry in high school, because I didn't like the smells. During the summer quarter of my freshman year, an accelerated course in chemistry was offered. That would be my only subject, and I would have my year of chemistry finished. To get it over with, Rosa Lee (a senior) and I immersed ourselves in chemistry mornings, afternoons, and evenings. It was a grueling experience! Sham and I called anything out of the ordinary an "experience". As we carried on with our lives as students, the war was an ever present thought in our minds, but there was no TV to keep us constantly reminded. We wrote lots of letters and looked forward to hearing from our friends in the service.

All was not classes, studying, and work at UT. We had dances with bands like Les Elgar, Jimmy & Tommy Dorsey. The dances were held in the university gymnasium. How excited I was the first time that I saw a revolving ball of little mirrors overhead! Sham and another friend talked me into joining her sorority. Actually I couldn't afford it, but I didn't think that I could continue in college much longer anyway. It would be an "experience"! My sorority experience turned out to be good for me. My sorority sisters amazed me when they chose me to be one of their members to represent them at the annual "Beauty Ball" and for Engineering Queen. I was so shy that if I would have had to say anything, I would have passed out when I was escorted out onto the stage at the ball. I would love to see a picture or movie of that!

All the while we knew that, in nearby Oak Ridge, something very secret was going on. People who were hired to work there were thoroughly checked for security. Most of them did not know what they were working on. A few years later, I would learn that my future husband, George, was working at Oak Ridge a short period of that time before joining the

It was not until 1945 when it was revealed to the public that the secret was the manufacture of the atomic bomb.

Navy. To get into Oak Ridge, a "pass" was necessary. Many of the buildings were temporary, and at first it seemed that mud or dry dirt was everywhere. Walkways were quickly constructed of wood. It was not until 1945 when it was revealed to the public that the secret was the manufacture of the atomic bomb. Today, Oak Ridge is a beautiful, modern city.

During my third quarter as a freshman, I had a live-in nanny job near the campus in the home of the niece of the president of the university, Dr. James Hoskins. Mrs. Creekmore's husband was away in the service, so her mother lived there, also. I went to classes as usual. My job was to help with two-year-old twins, Betsy & David. I was like their big sister & bathed them, read stories, took them for walks, and washed the supper dishes. It was exciting when Dr. Hoskins came over for dinner. I always took time out for the Saturday afternoon football games. General Neyland was the coach then, and I never saw the Vols lose a home game. As I recall, I received about $10 a week and was able to save most of it.

I missed my friends, so I moved back on campus the next quarter. A group of us girls lived upstairs in Tyson House, a big southern mansion which at that time was the Episcopal Student Center. It is now the alumni building. My typing skills got me a job as cashier in the university cafeteria. That job and additional typing carried me on until graduation. I did take a quarter off and went to Miami Beach where I had a cousin and worked as a live-in nanny again. This time was to care for two little girls. The family had a boat which made for some exciting times. One time we went fishing and I caught a 3 ft. barracuda! I have a picture to prove it.

Soon I learned that the Institute of Aviation Psychology of the Civil Aeronautics Administration was organized to conduct studies of instructional methods used in pilot training at the University of Tennessee. I applied for this program and was accepted. Again, I was required to have a parent's signature. This time, I convinced my wise Mama to give me permission. (Later on, after I learned to fly, Daddy bragged to his buddies that Geneva had learned to fly!) I was paired with another student, each of us to be trained by a different method. We were "guinea pigs". I never knew the identity of the other person. We received college credit and studied ground rules and received flying instructions. To write this story, I dug out my "Pilot's Log Book" so that I could recall specifically what I learned. Then I checked the name on the book to be sure that I really did that! Sure enough, it was me! The plane was a Piper Cub 0r J-3. With my instructor, we did all of the things that I would later do solo. After about 10½ hours of instructions, I did 20 minutes of solo take-offs and landings. After that, my solo flights were made up of more take-offs and landings, spot landings, steep turns, power-on landings, spins, spirals, and stalls for a total of 35½ hours. My instructor wanted me to continue and get my cross-country flying so that I could get a license. By that time, the war was winding down and my goals were different. I loved UT and wanted to graduate. Yes, I did catch rides to the airport several times. Just stand on the corner by the dorm and pretty soon a ride comes along. It was safe — at least we thought that it was. Times were different then!

The whole nation was shocked when President Roosevelt died suddenly on April 12, 1945. It was during an unprecedented fourth term. The general public would not know until years later that their president was in a wheel chair as a result of polio contracted when he was 39-years-old. Vice President Harry Truman became our president. The first reaction of some was that "he was just a haberdasher". Years before, he and a friend started a business together in Kansas City, but it failed, leaving him with debts of about $20,000. Rather than filing for bankruptcy, he paid every cent during the next ten years. He gained a reputation for being honest and eventually became a senator and then vice president. President Roosevelt had not consulted with him on major domestic and foreign policies since the election five months prior to his death. Vice President Truman was unprepared to become the president of a nation at war and had much to learn.

The plan for victory in Europe had been made and put into effect before Truman took office. On May 7, less than a month after taking office, President Truman announced the surrender of Germany. The war in Europe ended and the country was wild with excitement! Attention was then focused on the war in the Pacific. After six months of intense fire-bombing of 67 Japanese cities, followed by an ultimatum which was ignored by the Showa regime, President Truman authorized the virtual destruction of Hiroshima and Nagasaki by atomic bombs. The nuclear weapon "Little Boy" was dropped on Hiroshima on Monday, August 6, 1945 followed on August 9 by detonation of the "Fat Man" nuclear bomb over Nagasaki. Six days later, Japan announced its surrender to the Allied Powers, signing the "Instrument of Surrender" on September 2, officially ending the Pacific War and the ending of WWII. Again, there was much celebrating, honking of horns and yelling — except for those whose loved ones would not be coming home.

LIFE'S LESSON:

Being a teenaged Tennessee girl during WWII taught me many things. More than just learning to send telegrams and how to fly during wartime, I also learned honesty, how to work hard, how to treat others, how to be innovative, and how to make do with what we had.

Lesson 55

Turn Them Loose
or
Let Them Plot Their Own Doom

By Graham Swafford

*I*n this lesson, I'm going to deliver an observation that might be the best family relations' advice in my book. This advice is the hardest lesson in the entire book to follow.

It is difficult for a parent not to become involved and/or assert oneself (even when unwanted) when a child is involved. Some people cannot suppress their opinions on matters involving their children. I point out words spoken cannot be forgotten or withdrawn.

> *Over the years, Sharon and I have repeatedly seen well-meaning families bring unhappy, resistant children into family businesses, professions, etc., against the child's will, to disastrous results.*

Years ago, my sister Claudia moved to Memphis and thereafter became a misguided Episcopalian and a Democrat. My mother was not impressed. The joke around town was that my mother was going to take Claudia out of her will. My sister and her husband seem to have prospered beyond our wildest imagination. I am glad my sister is in Memphis prospering as a Democrat and an Episcopalian rather than in Marion County arguing with us. If you haven't guessed by now, my parents turned my sister loose.

Several years ago, when my son was in college, I called to give him instructions about courses to take, etc. to get into law school. My son told me repeatedly he did not particularly enjoy going to college and was trying to graduate as quickly as possible. About the 10th time my son told me that he was not at all interested in going to law school and sit on his posterior through three years of grinding boredom studying the common law, I had an epiphany moment of insight:

"I'm not going to drag you through law school then bring you back to Marion County and fight with you for the next 40 years."

My son now lives in Nashville, where he and his wife are happy and prospering. We turned him loose.

My daughter got a CPA designation and a law degree. Shelton now works for Joseph Decosimo, an institutional CPA firm in Chattanooga, specializing in estates. Shelton and her husband are happy and prospering. We turned her loose.

Over the years, Sharon and I have repeatedly seen well-meaning families bring unhappy, resistant children into family businesses, professions, etc., against the child's will, to disastrous results. I have seen absolutely heartbreaking situations brought about by wonderful people with the best of intentions trying to help those they loved more than anybody in the world.

LIFE'S LESSON:

Give your children every opportunity in the world; give them a world-class education; give them your unqualified love and support; give them a safe harbor of protection in which they can always retreat. Don't bad-mouth or ridicule your children publicly even when they are crazy. Then...

Turn them loose and let them plot their own doom!

Words cannot describe the difficulty of this lesson.

Lesson 56

An Ounce of Gall Will Get You Everywhere

By Shelton Swafford Chambers
Signal Mountain, Tenn.

When I was a little girl, my parents would always tell me that I could do anything I put my mind to. Quite frankly, I always assumed that I was completely capable of doing whatever I wanted to do. Alas, as I got older, that unquestioning optimism wavered a bit.

I would question whether I could really do something. Could I succeed in school? Could I pass the CPA exam? Could I do what I wanted to do?

My dad would always shrug my questions off and say "Shel, an ounce of gall will get you everywhere." What does that even mean?! I discovered the true meaning not long ago…

My cousin Cameron was off in Afghanistan. Not knowing anything else to do to support his efforts, I decided that I needed to send him regular notes, but those got old quickly. So, I decided to take a picture of Cameron that I found on Facebook, enlarge it and print it out. My goal was to take it along with me everywhere I went and take pictures of the picture of Cameron at various locations. Then, I could send those pictures to Cameron so he'd see where all he went the past few weeks.

A few weeks into the project, I went to a dinner where Serena and Venus Williams were the speakers. They were waaaaay up at the front of the room, and I was waaaaaaaaaaaaaaay in the back. After dinner, they were supposed to take pictures with a few of the VIPs in attendance, and then be whisked away. Needless to say, I was NOT considered one of the VIPs worthy of a glamour shot with the Williams sisters.

I was convinced, however, that getting Cameron's picture with the Williams sister would be the ultimate triumph! I mean, if I could get them to pose with Cameron's picture, that would be the absolute best surprise for him to get! The only problem was how to get access to them.

They had plenty of people surrounding them. The line to get to them was pretty guarded. This was going to be tricky! I considered giving up and just holding his little picture up in their general vicinity, but I tried several shots and it just looked lame. No, that wouldn't work!

Before I knew it, the Williams sisters were finished with their pictures and they were being taken behind the scenes. I had lost my chance. Or had I? I noticed that after they went behind the curtains, all the security kind of relaxed. Were they still behind there? Could I sneak behind there? I decided to go for it.

I ever so nimbly climbed over the ropes and quickly scampered across the red carpet. Then, I started walking toward the small opening in the curtain to get behind the scenes. I walked liked I belonged there — with purpose and all the confidence of someone that belonged there. As people watched, I just brushed them aside as if I knew exactly where I was going. Finally! I was behind the scenes. I knew that I had to quickly find the Williams sisters, get my picture, and pop out of there. I spotted the two sisters down the hall a little and knew the time to act was here. As I passed by the event organizers and others, I squared my shoulders and confidently called out to them. As they turned to see who was calling their name, I walked right up to them, handed them the picture and said "this is my cousin Cam, who is fighting in Afghanistan. He'd like a picture with you, so say cheese." They looked at me with a bewildered look, and I again encouraged them to smile so I could take their picture. Not knowing what else to do, the Williams sisters took Cameron's picture, gave me a big smile and let me take their picture. Not wanting to push my luck, I quickly took my picture back, thanked the sisters, and made my exit. As I left, someone came up to me and asked what I was doing back there, and I replied that I must have gotten lost somehow, and quickly hurried off.

> *My dad would always shrug my questions off and say 'Shel, an ounce of gall will get you everywhere.' What does that even mean?!*

However, victory was mine — I had gotten the picture! While I had some concerns that this could not be done, I put my mind to it, acted like it was the most natural thing for me to be doing, and ran right into the Williams sisters in time for a picture.

LIFE'S LESSON:

My dad was right — an ounce of gall will *get you everywhere!*

Board of Directors

By Graham Swafford

*L*et me make this lesson short and to the point. I will avoid entertaining examples.

Being invited to sit on a board of directors or commission is typically an invitation to become a "potted plant."

Being invited to sit on a board of directors or commission is typically an invitation to become a 'potted plant.'

I have been on several boards during my lifetime. As a young attorney being invited to serve on a board or commission was an ego thing that I fell for every time, generally to my detriment.

If you do not know why you are invited to sit on a board of directors along with what is expected of you, you should decline the invitation promptly without hesitation.

If you cannot clearly articulate why you want to sit on a particular board or commission in less than five seconds then promptly decline the offer without hesitation.

If you are on a board of directors with a group of people who ignore the obvious, plead ignorance about the obvious, look the other way and/or lack curiosity then "get off the board" every time.

LIFE'S LESSON:

If you don't know why you are asked to serve on a board of directors or if you cannot promptly state your purpose for being on the board of directors then you should refuse.

I repeat — the response to an invitation to be on a board of directors should typically be — Emphatically No!

Remember Who They Are
and Where You Found Them

By Graham Swafford

*Y*ears ago on a cold blistery day, a kind Indian brave was walking down a path and found a large snake almost frozen to death.

The Indian brave, being a kind-hearted soul, gently picked up the snake and took him to his teepee where the snake was revived, fattened and given a prominent position in the brave's family. The snake prospered. The snake was loved.

'Why did you do that to me? We were so good to you! We loved you!'

The Indian brave and his family always treated the snake with kindness and affection. The snake truly became one of the family.

One night, for absolutely no reason and without any provocation whatsoever, the snake lunged at the brave who had saved his life and bit him. As life was slipping away from the Indian brave with poisonous venom running through his veins he looked at the snake and with a heartbroken gasp cried out "Why did you do that to me? We were so good to you! We loved you!"

To which the snake replied with a chuckle and a smile, "You knew I was a snake … You knew where you found me."

LIFE'S LESSON:

Remember who or what they are … Remember where you found them!

Remembering My Dad … and Stan the Man

By Bill Haltom
Memphis, Tenn.

*I*t was the happiest day of a very happy childhood. And I owe it to two men — my father and Stan the Man.

It was a summer day in 1959. My father took me to Sportsman's Park in St. Louis where we saw the Cardinals play the Milwaukee Braves. To this day, over a half century later, I can close my eyes and relive almost every moment of that glorious sunlit day.

In my mind's eye, I can see the image of the crowds filing into the ballpark. I had never seen so many people.

> *On that glorious day nearly 54 years ago, I could not find words to describe it. Watching Stan the Man circle the bases was pure joy.*

I can visualize the moment when my father took me by the hand and led me up a ramp to the section where our seats were located. I can still see the image of my father dressed in his business suit (in those days, men wore suits and ties and hats, even to ballgames) and my mother in a pretty summer dress.

I remember the incredible scene of the diamond and the outfield. I remember the vivid colors — green and brown and white. It was breath-taking.

I remember the giant "Budweiser" scoreboard in left field. I marveled at how I could watch the scores of all the major league games in progress that day.

I remember the Cardinals taking the field as the crowd cheered, and I remember the sound of the organist playing jaunty songs.

Believe it or not, I actually remember the name of the starting pitcher for the Cardinals. Ernie Broglio. A few seasons later, he would be traded to the Cubs for Lou Brock in the greatest trade for all time for the Cardinals and the worst trade of all time for the Cubs.

I remember having a hot dog and a Coca-Cola. To this day, it's probably the greatest meal I've ever experienced.

I remember standing during the seventh inning stretch and singing "Take Me Out to the Ballgame" with my mom and dad.

But above all, I remember the most wonderful moment of a wonderful day.

In the bottom of the ninth, with the Cardinals trailing by a run, number 6, Stan the Man Musial, came to the plate with a fellow Redbird on first base. I remember Stan in the batter's box, standing tall, holding his bat straight up in the air. I remember a swing and a crack. And then I remember watching the ball sail into the right-field seats.

It was what is now called a walk-off home run. But on that glorious day nearly 54 years ago, I could not find words to describe it. Watching Stan the Man circle the bases was pure joy.

I thought about that magical day recently when I heard the news that Stan the Man had passed away at the age of 92. Shortly thereafter, I visited my 88 year-old father in the nursing facility where he now resides.

"Dad," I asked him, "do you remember that day when I was a little boy and you and Mom took me to Sportsman's Park, and we saw Stan Musial hit that home run in the bottom of the ninth?"

Dad didn't say anything. He stared at me for a moment, and then he nodded and smiled.

And I smiled too.

LIFE'S LESSON:
There is nothing like the bond you have when sharing special memories with loved ones.

Elections Make a Difference

By Graham Swafford

*T*he following is a political lesson.

Good policies make a difference. Good governance (either in corporations and/or politically) make all the difference in the world.

Over the years, I have had a stream of people come into my office and want me to sue the government, some governmental agency or governmental subdivision because of some perceived wrong.

At one time or the other I have had folks come in and want me to sue the road commissioner, the school system, the mayor, the sheriff, the public library, the state of Tennessee and the governor, the United States of America, not to mention the president of the United States and Congress.

> *I think proper society needs to be sued and sued often.*

You name them — I have had an opportunity to sue them. I have an appetite to sue some of these folks. I offer no defense to the fact that I am discontented and have an appetite to sue the status quo.

I think proper society needs to be sued and sued often. I can assure my readers there is not a litigation crisis but if there is a problem, it is because people who know better don't file enough lawsuits.

Having vented my spleen on the subject more times than not, people want me to file lawsuits against a governmental entity just because they are not happy with the "direction things are going not to mention garden-variety incompetency."

Folks, let me be very clear. Let me express a fundamental proposition of law. General unhappiness and garden-variety dissatisfaction with the direction government is going does not make a lawsuit, regardless of the facts.

Typically about 95 percent of the time when somebody comes in and wants me to sue a governmental entity I tell them as a matter of law they simply have no cause of action.

Once again, for those who might be a little confused — the fact the government is inefficient, schools are bad, economic development is nonexistent, the planning commission is incompetent, the county commission is asleep at the wheel, there is absolutely no oversight or whatever, as a matter of law, to allow you to *sue the incompetents!*

Repeatedly I tell people every two or four years there is an "election." I encourage people to become involved in politics.

If you are interested in good government become a Democrat, a Republican, an Independent or join the Tea Party. These are all fine organizations.

Support candidates who have your sympathy. More important, "give candidates you support a political contribution.

LIFE'S LESSONS:

If you are unhappy with the way things are going, show a little spine — raise Cain. Become a participant — get involved! Elections send messages and make a difference.

The Mindless Herd

By Graham Swafford

First they came for the communist,
and I did not speak out because I wasn't a communist.
Then they came for the trade unionists,
and I did not speak out because I wasn't a trade unionists.
Then they came for the Jews,
and I did not speak out because I wasn't a Jew.
Then they came for me
and there was no one left to speak out for me.
— *Martin Niemoller, a former German pastor**

> **70 percent of the people are nothing more than the mindless herd — sheep waiting to be told what to do.**

I have always been bewildered by the acquiescence of the German people prior to World War II. We generally think of the Germans as "folks sort of like us." We generally share with the German people the same religion, same background, etc. We just have a lot in common. The Germans are good people whom I generally admire, but then the German nation brought us the most deadly if not profoundly evil war in the history of the world. Millions were killed as a result of the evil of World War II.

LIFE'S LESSON:

With the above background in mind, I make the following observation or life lesson:

15 percent of the people in the world are so silly they will support, follow and believe anything regardless of how crazy and unfounded.

15 percent of the people are opposed to everything. These people are so negative they will oppose going to the rapture or doing what is in their best interest. These people are crazy!

70 percent of the people are nothing more than the mindless herd — sheep waiting to be told what to do and/or stamped-

ed. These people have the greatest potential for good and evil and at times can be the most dangerous! These are the quickest to go to war.

Comment: I suppose the above observation is a little cynical. Some of my readers might find the observation offensive. I make no apology. You cannot convince me that I am incorrect in my assessment.

I don't care if my children consider me a tad bit eccentric. I would hope that my children (and especially my grandchildren) never consider me to be a part of the mindless herd and I carry the same expectations for them.

*Martin Niemoller was a German pastor and theologian born in Lippstadt, Germany, in 1892. Niemoller was an anti-communist and supported Hitler's rise to power but when Hitler insisted on the supremacy of the state over religion, Niemoller became disillusioned. He became the leader of a group of German clergymen opposed to Hitler. Unlike Niemoller, they gave in to the Nazis' threats. In 1937 Niemoller was arrested and eventually confined in the Sachsenhausen and Dachau concentration camps. Niemoller's crime was "not being enthusiastic enough about the Nazi movement." Niemoller was released in 1945 by the Allies. Niemoller continued his career in Germany as a clergyman and as a leading voice of penance and reconciliation for the German people after World War II. His statement, sometimes presented as a poem, is well-known, frequently quoted, and is a popular model for describing the dangers of political apathy, as it often begins with specific and targeted fear and hatred, which soon escalates out of control.

Lesson 62

We Become What We Think

By Dr. Nell W. Mohney
Chattanooga, Tenn.

*T*here are six words that I wish I had learned and understood early in my life. They would have improved my life immeasurably in my perception, in personal happiness and in success in every faucet of life. Those six words are: "You become what you think about." It is the key to success or failure.

Philosophers, psychologists, teachers, religious leaders have disagreed about many things through the years, but they all seem to be in agreement about this. For example, it was Marcus Aurelius, the great Roman emperor who said, "A man's life is what his thoughts make it." William Shakespeare wrote: "Our doubts are traitors, and oft make us lose the good we might win, by fearing to attempt."

In our own county the beloved author and philosopher, Ralph Waldo Emerson, wrote "A person is what he or she thinks about all day long." It was William James who declared: "The greatest discovery of my generation is that human beings can alter their lives by altering their attitude of mind."

Charles Swindoll, well-known Christian author and minister wrote: "The longer I live, the more I realize the impact of attitude on life. To me, attitude is more important than facts. It is more important than the past, than education, than money, than circumstances, than failures, than successes, than what other people say or do. It is more important than appearance, giftedness or skill. It will make or break a company, a church, a home."

The remarkable thing is we have a choice every day regarding the attitude we will embrace that day. We cannot change the fact that people will act in a certain way, we cannot change the inevitable. The only thing we can do is play on the one string we have and that is our attitude. I am convinced that life is 10 percent what happens to me and 90 percent how I react to it. And so it is with you. We are in charge of our attitudes.

How does all this work? It was the late Early Nightingale, the great motivator of business and professional people, who helped me see clearly what my Christian faith had taught me; namely, that thoughts are living things. They are powerful because, when consistently held, they become attitudes. Thoughts and attitudes determine belief; beliefs determine character, and character determines destiny. He also reminded us that we have the power to choose our thoughts.

As an illustration, he suggested that the mind is somewhat like an acre of land on which a farmer can plant a crop like corn, or a deadly poison like nightshade. The land doesn't care what we plant, but will give us back in abundance what we plant. Mr. Nightingale suggested that the mind, though far more complex and creative than the fallow land, is similar in that what we put in we get out. If we sow negative or evil thoughts, we will get negative or evil results. If we sow positive or constructive thoughts, we will get positive or constructive results.

The remarkable thing is we have a choice every day regarding the attitude we will embrace that day.

The Bible certainly confirms this in numerous places, three of which are: "As a man thinks within himself so is he. (Proverbs 23:7); "Whatever a man sows, this he shall also reap" (Galatians 6:7); "Whatever is true, whatever is honorable, whatever is right, whatever is pure, whatever is lovely, whatever is good report, if there is any excellence or anything worthy of praise, think on these things" (Philippians 4:8).

An illustration of how thoughts can be turned into dreams and beliefs is the story of Jesse Owen who grew up in Cleveland, Ohio, in a home which he described as "materially poor, but spiritually rich." Charlie Paddock, a great athlete and one often described as "the fastest human being alive," came to speak at Jesse's school. He said to the kids: "Listen! What do you want to be? You name it and believe that God will help you be that."

Young Jesse Owen thought to himself: "I want to be what Mr. Paddock has been. I want to be the fastest human being on Earth." Rushing from the auditorium to the gymnasium, he said exuberantly to his coach: "I have a dream! I have a dream!" The coach replied "It's great to have a dream, Jesse, but you have to build a ladder to your dreams. The first rung on the ladder is determination, the second is dedication, the third is discipline and the fourth is attitude."

The result of Jesse Owen's thoughts, dreams, attitudes and beliefs are well-known. He was the fastest man to ever run the 100 meter dash, and the fastest man ever to run the 200 meter dash. His broad jump record lasted for 24 years. He won four gold medals in the Berlin Olympic Games and his name was included in the Charter List in the American Hall of Athletic Fame.

LIFE'S LESSON:

Remember that we become what we think. Thoughts are powerful because they determine attitudes, belief and character. Jesus summarized it succinctly when He said: "If you can believe, all things are possible to him who believes." (Mark 9:23)

Depression

By Graham Swafford

E very year, particularly in January or February, I have someone, considered to be a solid sort of person, hire me to represent them regarding a personal problem. The business is predictable. I usually have several of these cases.

The personal problem for which I am hired usually involves a divorce, DUI, assault, financial matter, etc. I stress these clients are not your typical garden-variety outlaws.

Problems with depression can torture individuals for a lifetime and impact families for generations.

More often than not, I have noticed the problems these clients have are usually brought about and/or were exacerbated by some form of mental depression.

I can write books about fine people who do things totally out-of-character which is brought about by drugs, alcohol, etc., all exacerbated or made worse by depression. Words cannot express the shame and embarrassment these folks feel.

The real tragedy is the fact that these problems are not only embarrassing to the client but are extremely damaging (if not life altering) to the client's family.

I am of the opinion that depression is as much a medical condition as a broken leg or a common cold. Usually people recover from some type of medical condition or at least they mercifully die. Problems with depression can torture individuals for a lifetime and impact families for generations.

There has been so much written about depression in the last few years you would think modern science just discovered it.

Depression has been around for centuries. Abraham Lincoln (who I consider the country's greatest president) suffered from profound depression. Winston Churchill (who I consider the greatest leader of the 20th century, not to mention saved western civilization) called depression "being bit by the black dog."

I understand depression.

LIFE'S LESSON:

If you suffer from depression, don't be embarrassed or ashamed to get help — you are in good company. Bouts of depression, if not addressed or treated, have the potential to take you and/or your family places you do not dream.

Regrets and Read to Your Children

By Graham Swafford

J don't have many regrets.

If I harbored a regret, I would not be inclined to make an admission and/or confession.

Folks, this is not Facebook.

Sadly, not many people understand the phrase "taking secrets to the grave."

There are some things, however, I wish I could redo. When my children were young, I wish I had read more to them. Read anything to your children and grandchildren — good literature, bad literature, the National Enquirer, the Bible, it does not matter.

At one time, my daughter Shelton and I would retire to my library and read the National Enquirer and the Globe. Sharon thought we were reading trash, but we loved the imagination and the literary talent set forth in these magazines. We had a great time. Sharon was furious and never understood.

When my children were young, I wish I had read more to them. Read anything to your children and grandchildren — good literature, bad literature, the National Enquirer, the Bible, it does not matter.

LIFE'S LESSON:

Read to your children!

Along with the National Enquirer for literary excellence and imagination, I would recommend reading to your children Hurlbut's "Story of the Bible."

Honoring to God/The Little Old Church

By Allison Buchanan
South Pittsburg, Tenn.

s a young child growing up with three brothers (Kevin, Chris and Kelby Ferrell), l was a bit spoiled with love. I am not sure if it's because I was the only girl or that I was just so loveable; I would say so loveable. My parents, Roy and Linda Ferrell, always put God first and taught us strong Christian morals. We were a close family that always had fun together, except when my brother Chris, who is the most competitive of the four siblings, would lose in any game we might play. We were the typical Christian family who always went to church and loved to help others.

As a child I remember my father being the provider of the household. After working long hours he would still find the time to spend with his family. On a daily basis he would eat dinner with us every night, coach his sons' teams, play with me, and most importantly he showed my mother love and respect. Meanwhile, my mother cleaned the house, cooked three meals a day, read her Bible regularly, and was always there for her children. I can't ever remember a time they weren't involved with our activities. My family was not rich with money, obviously, with one income providing for six people, but we were rich in love. No matter how hard times got for my parents, they always kept their faith in God. I was baptized as a young girl and understood exactly what I was doing, but I had no idea the trials I would be faced with later in life.

In high school I was the friend that no one wanted to go out with on Friday night, due to my early curfew of 10:30, when everything was just starting to get good. Who would want to leave and take me home? You can imagine the names I had for my parents. I would call them old fashioned, goody-goody, too protective, or say they were too churchy. My friends would laugh and talk about how strict my parents were, but when they had a problem, my parents were who they went to. Looking back on all my complaints, I see the valuable lessons they were teaching.

In college I started falling off my Christian path. I was making horrible decisions, running with the wrong crowds, and staying away from my parents so they wouldn't pressure me into going to church. Soon I realized that Jesus was in my heart, so I was feeling the guilt and pressure anyway. I had many talks with God about "not doing it again." Thank you, God, for never giving up on me when I know you could. My mother later told me of all the nights she prayed for me. The big picture was that through all my wrong doings, my parents continued to show me Christian love.

I married Steven Buchanan and started turning my focus back on God. Shortly after marriage, I had my first child, Blake Buchanan. All the Biblical teachings my parents were trying to teach were starting to make more sense. A child does change everything. Church started becoming a bigger priority, and I was making better choices in my life. I will never forget the moment I rededicated my life to the Lord. I was in Mt. Zion Church in Shelbyville, Tenn., listening to the words Terrell "Doe" Buchanan sang about "The Little Old Church." The words of the song touched my heart and from that day forward, I live to honor God. I had my second child, Bentley Buchanan, and was studying God's word regularly. It's amazing the difference God made in my life. God brings happiness. I can't begin to thank God for the wonderful parents he gave me.

LIFE'S LESSON:
The life lessons my parents taught are to put God first and honor him in everything I do. When Christians ask the question: "Would God be pleased?," it makes the answer easier.

The Little Old Church
As I sit here and let my mind role back
I can see a little old church
Sitting by the railroad tracks
It's a shabby old place
Where we use to sing "Amazing Grace"
Talking about a good time
A mighty, mighty good time.
Well my mother
She use to take me there
She sat me on her knee
And took me to the Lord in prayer.
We sang "Amazing Grace"
At that Halleluiah place
Talking about a good time yea
A mighty, mighty good time.
People use to put up a tent
In an open field
Folks would come from miles around
Traveling over rocks and hills
Very little money was raised
But many, many soul was saved
Talking about a good time yea
A mighty, mighty good time.

Find the Throne and
Get to Know Who is Sitting on It

By Graham Swafford

*T*his next lesson will be short but possibly priceless advice for the young and ambitious.

This lesson, standing alone for some, might be worth the price of the entire book. For some, this lesson might be worth "millions."

> *It is better to be well-connected than brilliant.*

The lesson is incredibly simple — "wherever you find yourself in this world, find the throne quick (the first thing) and become a friend with the person sitting on the throne."

I am embarrassed to say that I did not realize the importance of this lesson until I was in my mid-50s. I am convinced most people go through life and the significance of this lesson *never* crosses their mind.

When I was a young man, I was dispatched to the University of Tennessee. I never met the president of the University of Tennessee or even knew where his office was located. The board of trustees at the university never thought to invite me to sit in the sky box nor did they know I existed. If I had died at the university I am convinced there would have been no acknowledgment or expression of concern.

I was an officer in the United States Army stationed at Aberdeen, Maryland and it never crossed my mind to ask who the commanding officer of the base was nor did I know where command headquarters was located. I can say my contribution to the defense of the Republic was quickly forgotten by a grateful nation.

While I cannot say I had a bad time in college or in the Army (I really had a great time), I think a fair statement is there were moments of frustrating non-productivity. Later in life, I had an epiphany moment that arrived with such clarity I was embarrassed. So for the young, smart and ambitious, the following is "Life's Lesson."

LIFE'S LESSON:

Wherever life takes you, whatever you do, the first thing you should do is "Find the THRONE and personally get to know who is sitting on it"! If you don't fine the THRONE and if you don't know who is sitting on it, you will be limited. It is better to be well-connected than brilliant.

I taught the above lesson to my children from day one.

Everybody's Got a Price — Everybody's Got a Story

By Graham Swafford

*S*everal years ago, to great fanfare, the state of Tennessee implemented the Tennessee Educational Lottery.

I don't mean to sound like a self-righteous, fuddy-duddy moralist but, quite frankly, I just don't think as a matter of public policy, state government should get into the gambling business.

$65 million caught the attention of Graham Swafford from Marion County.

I felt from the "get go" the lottery was nothing more than a scheme to tax people who did not understand the simplest of math. A person has a greater chance of getting hit by lightning than winning the lottery. To this day, I believe the lottery was wrong and feel it takes advantage of vulnerable people.

My views were neither consulted nor shared by the public. Apparently, I am the only person in Tennessee who disapproves of the lottery.

One night I was watching television and there was a news flash. I love news flashes. A good news flash always captures my curiosity. I have never ignored a news flash.

The news flash, on this particular evening, revealed the lottery was having a drawing that very night and the winner would receive $65 million.

$65 million caught the attention of Graham Swafford from Marion County.

At that moment I looked over at Sharon and told her I was going to buy some lottery tickets and asked if she would like to join me. Sharon refused to accompany me.

I went over to Wildwood and the line of those buying lottery tickets went all the way to the highway. It was an enjoyable evening where I met many new, not to mention interesting friends. The truth of the matter is I had a lot of fun with my new gambling buddies.

LIFE'S LESSON:

So here is "Life's Lesson," which I believe is true for everyone — I repeat — everyone:

Every person has a price. Every person has a story. Every person has a button that, if pushed, can motivate them for good or for evil.

There is nothing more that can be said about this trait.

Everything Happens for a Reason

By Phil Colquette
Gulf Shores, Ala.

*W*hen Graham asked me to write a story in his book, the only instruction he gave me was "don't write a Graham Swafford story."

I can assure you, the world is rich with "Graham Swafford" stories.

As I was preparing to write my life lesson, I was reminded of fond memories, not to mention great stories.

I remember the time we were in Joe Story's geometry class at South Pittsburg High School taking a test. Mr. Story said that he would allow Norris Hall, Gary Elledge and me to pool our efforts together and then we would add up our score for a total grade. The three of us still failed the test.

I remember the Boy Scout camping trips. Not to mention Graham Swafford, but he and I are the only individuals that ever went all the way through the scouting program and never started a campfire. We had a scout in Troop 63 named Ric Ivey. Ric was a world-class pyro man. Ric could start a fire on a flat rock in the middle of the Atlantic Ocean. I remember arriving at the Boy Scout campsite and Graham would look over and say "Rickem, start the fire" and within minutes we would all be enjoying a roaring campfire. In Boy Scouts we also learned you could wedge a cigarette in the opening of a pull tab on a soda can and you could then smoke a cigarette in our tent without the glow. We took magazines on these camping trips and I am happy to report we learned about the female anatomy.

The stories of growing up in South Pittsburg are endless, memorable and perhaps best kept secrets by lifelong friends all to be taken to the grave.

Let me tell you my life lesson:

Several months ago, I was looking at my old diary. The year 1971 had been a rough year. My friend, Norris Hall and I had gone to Cleveland, Tenn., where I had the hots to buy a red Fiat Spider. I drove the vehicle happily away and thereafter, the next happy day in my life was when I sold the darn car. Repair bills came one after another.

In August of 1971, Dick Ryan and I were involved in an automobile accident on Sweetens Cove Road. We were both hospitalized for a week.

My father had a classic Ford 7-liter automobile which was stolen off the parking lot at the high school.

If all had not gone well in 1971, I broke up with my girlfriend which I suppose could be a topic of another life lesson, probably best left untold.

In the early part of 1971, I was injured at an after-school job and taken to Erlanger Hospital as a result of serious injuries. I lay in the hospital bed for a week totally blind.

The above experiences were just typical examples of a horrible year where it was apparent I was going nowhere.

As I lay in the hospital with my eyes shut, not to mention scared to death, I had that epiphany moment. I knew I needed a change of scenery. I guess I know how the Apostle Paul felt on the Damascus Road when he was knocked blind.

> *As I lay in the hospital with my eyes shut, not to mention scared to death, I had that epiphany moment.*

Somewhere during this time frame my old buddy, Graham, talked me into going with him to sell books for the Southwestern Company of Nashville. I needed a change of scenery. Certainly selling books for the Southwestern Company beat going to Vietnam.

When I got out on the book field it suddenly dawned on me that the money was pretty good and by the way I am pretty good at this selling.

I sold books for the Southwestern Company for three years. The Southwestern Company increased my confidence. After college (which included not the greatest academic record) I got a job with the Yellow Page Company. I was able to start my own directory publishing company, Gulf Publishing. I have been married to the same woman for 35 years. Life has been a great success. I am a fortunate man. I could have easily taken a different path. So the following is my "Life Lesson."

LIFE'S LESSON

I credit my mother, Mae Colquette, for putting this lesson into words: "Everything happens for a reason."

Team Players

By Randy Kinnard
Nashville, Tenn.

I am a jury lawyer, also known as a trial lawyer. I have been representing patients and their families in medical malpractice cases in Tennessee for over three decades. Here is the story of my worst moment ever in court:

I was representing an 8-year-old boy in circuit court in Nashville. He had been injured due to the alleged negligence of his pediatrician. Winning medical malpractice cases is hard. National statistics show that about 80 percent of the cases that go to trial are lost by the patient.

Because these cases are difficult enough to begin with, I do not want to do anything to make matters more challenging. I do not want to give a jury the wrong impression about me, and so I dress very conservatively, usually wearing clothes that do not "shout" at the jury. I have a theory that if you wear clothes that might offend one juror, you can lose that juror on something other than the merits of the case.

With very rare exceptions, in medical malpractice cases, the plaintiff (person bringing the lawsuit) must present medical testimony through expert witnesses to show that the doctor charged with malpractice has violated the standard of care and caused an injury to the patient. Without the appropriate expert testimony, the plaintiff cannot win the case.

I searched literature and found one of the nation's best-rated pediatricians from Atlanta. I called him on the phone and he agreed to review the case. I sent him the materials and records. He reviewed it all and said the child had a meritorious case and he would be happy to testify against the doctor in Nashville. The expert gave a deposition to the defense attorney and explained all the ways the defendant had violated pediatric standards.

The expert and I met for three hours the night before trial and went over his testimony. He confirmed the half-dozen ways the pediatrician had violated the standard of care. The expert was ready.

The next morning, the judge asked me to call the next witness. With great pride, stretching to my full six feet two inches, I said, "I am happy to, your Honor." I went into the hall, found the doctor sitting next to the courtroom door, and told him to come on in.

The doctor was sworn in, took his seat, and I started asking him the basic background questions about his qualifications — where he had practiced, how long he had been a pediatrician, whether he was board certified, etc. His credentials were superior and I could tell that the jury was impressed.

Eventually, I came to the question that is all-important for the plaintiff. The question and answers went like this:

"Doctor, have you reviewed the medical records carefully in this case?"

The doctor said, "Yes, sir, I have. Very carefully."

"And doctor, do you have an opinion as to whether or not the defendant doctor, seated over there, lived up to the standards of care, or violated them?"

"Yes, sir, I have formed such an opinion."

Knowing that the expert had told me many times in preparation about how badly the defendant doctor had violated the standard of care, I

> *At this moment I wished that a huge hole would open up in the courtroom floor and I could fall into it and disappear.*

looked at the jury in anxious anticipation of the home run we were about to hit. At which time, the doctor gave the following answer:

"This doctor lived up to the standard of care in every way."

After removing the dagger from my chest, I managed to say, "Doctor, I think you misunderstood my question. Let me repeat the question. Tell us whether or not this defendant doctor *violated the standard of care.*"

"I just told you. He lived up the standard of care in every way."

At this moment I wished that a huge hole would open up in the courtroom floor and I could fall into it and disappear. There was dead silence in the courtroom.

I looked up at the judge and said, "Your Honor, at this time, the plaintiff takes a voluntary dismissal of his case." (This is lawyer talk for the fact that the plaintiff's lawyer has elected to dismiss his client's case, preserving the right of the client to refile his case — if he can, ever find another lawyer to do so. A voluntary dismissal beats the court dismissing it as a matter of law.)

The judge nodded, smiled slightly, and said, "I can see why."

As everyone left the courtroom, I took the Atlanta doctor aside and said, "Doctor, what are you doing?"

He said, "What do you mean, what I am doing? I'm testifying."

"*Why* did you say the defendant had lived up to the standard of care?"

With a confused look, the doctor looked at me and said, "Well, you do represent the defendant doctor, don't you?"

"No!" I said. "I represent the patient."

The doctor replied, "Oh, I thought you were a defense lawyer. You dress like one."

LIFE'S LESSON

Always make sure you're playing on the same team. Be sure no one on your team has Alzheimer's disease.

Don't Let It Happen Again

By Graham Swafford

J learned the next lesson from John Hewgley, an old friend from South Pittsburg, Tenn. This is a short lesson but, for some, this lesson could be a priceless gift.

Periodically in the game of life, somebody simply "stabs you in the back." Trust me, a good deliberate, indiscriminate back stabbing happens to all of us at one time or another.

> *Trust me, 'a good deliberate, indiscriminate back stabbing' happens to all of us at one time or another.*

Nothing is more bonding and develops friendship like a good common back stabbing. The Bible teaches the importance of forgiveness so, of course, you should follow Biblical instructions after a good intentional back stabbing.

On the other hand, "never forget" and "never let them do it to you again."

LIFE'S LESSON:

From John Hewgley: If you stab me in the back once — shame on you ... If you stab me in the back twice — shame on me.

Never turn your back.

I thank John for this advice.

Etiquette of Bringing a Dog in a Salon/Day Spa

By Allison Buchanan
South Pittsburg, Tenn.

Those of you who know Graham Swafford will agree that he is one of a kind. He told the story about Joe Ray Wilson and the valuable lesson Joe taught him about apologizing and smiling to weasel your way out of any bad situation that may occur. I was at Studio 306 working on a Saturday morning. Those of you who make hair appointments understand that Saturday is a busy day in the salon. I noticed Graham walking in and going to the front desk to make an appointment. The next thing I saw was a big dog run past me and headed to the back where clients sit in hooded dryers. The dog continued to make himself at home in the back area. Everyone looked at me, and I asked Graham if that was his service dog, because if not he is going to have to get him out. That is the only type dog allowed in a salon. He asked me where the dog went, and I jokingly said, "He is probably in my office using the bathroom." Graham said, "Oh, no, he would never do that, not my dog." By that time the dog had made his way back up front to his owner and they proceeded to leave. Everyone laughed at the thought of Graham not even thinking anything about bringing his dog into a professional salon where clients were relaxing on their day off.

> *'Golly, I'll never do that again.'*

About five minutes after Graham left Tisha Gravitt, senior stylist, went to the back to mix more color and screamed out, "Oh, my!" I didn't even look that way. I knew exactly what that yell was for. Graham's dog had left a large pile in the middle of our floor. I had to stop what I was doing and clean up the mess.

Connie Ferrell, our front desk coordinator, took a picture of the massive pile to show Graham when he came back later that afternoon for his appointment.

When Graham arrived for his 1 p.m. appointment, I let him have it. I told him what kind of mess his dog had made in our floor. Graham immediately started denying the accusation and said his dog would never do anything like that. I got the picture to prove to Graham that it was on the floor. As soon as he saw the picture, he said, "Oh, no, that *is* my dog's mess," and flashed a big smile. "I am so, so sorry; it won't happen again," and flashed another big smile. He repeated at least three times, "Golly, I'll never do that again," and continued to flash a smile. The only thing different that Graham said that day that Joe Ray didn't teach him was "Please don't tell Sharon," so I promised I would not tell her and flashed a big smile.

LIFE'S LESSON:

Smiling and apologizing to weasel your way out of a situation works both ways.

*Note: The dog was Sassy.

No Profiles in Courage
or
A World Class Education

By Graham Swafford

இ

he following "Life's Lesson" will amuse some of my readers — others it will make absolutely furious.

Let me give you a little background. In the past, I have known people who have acquired "world class" formal educations, but don't have a speck of common sense. A fancy formal education from a prestigious school, with no practical knowledge, is absolutely worthless.

> *In the past, I have known people who have acquired 'world class' formal educations, but don't have a speck of common sense.*

Not to brag, but I know people who have graduated and/or received Ph.D.'s from the finest, most prestigious schools in the entire world. I have known people who have spent hundreds of thousands of dollars pursuing academic degrees from famous schools, but lack practical knowledge. Borrowing a line from Harry Truman: "This education is not worth 'warm spit'."

I'm not criticizing world class prestigious schools. Few things have been more important in my life and the life of my family than the fact that my sister and I were afforded great educations.

On the other hand, if a person is interested in obtaining a real, practical education, don't go to one of those "high-brow" colleges — save your money! Get on the county commission.

Simply stated, if you are interested in politics or how the world runs, "run for the county commission." The county commission is the greatest education in the entire world.

In the first place, there is very little oversight on the county commission. In the second place, there is absolutely no accountability on the county commission. Typically, county commissioners can get away with absolutely anything. There is no education and/or intellectual requirement for being on the county commission — you can be on the county commission and not know how to read. An understanding of good public policy is absolutely non-existent on the county commission. When asked difficult questions all a county commissioner has to say is "they never told us about that" and then look bewildered and dumb — works every time!

However...

Once you get on the county commission, a priceless education begins — on the county commission you learn about psychology, you learn about human nature, you learn a little math or all the essential math one needs to know (i.e. counting votes), you learn about governance, you learn about getting along and charm school, you learn a little mortuary science (i.e. where the skeletons are buried). Simply stated, you get a world class education (worth far more than any Ph.D. from an Ivy League School) on how the world works and how to "play the game."

LIFE'S LESSON:

If you want a real education or if you are interested in politics, run for the county commission!

Greed:
The Most Constant Human Emotion
By John David Brundige
Martin, Tenn.

Proverbs 16:11 — The Lord demands fairness in every business deal. He established this principle. The Living Bible Version.

*M*y experience in life is that there is an element of mankind that knows how they're going to take advantage of you before they ever shake hands on "the deal." They have it in their minds that life is a game and they're going to win the game with you. Fairness, honesty, integrity and "fairness in every business deal" is not understood by these folks. It's a game of "I win and you lose and that's how I view my business dealings in life. You're going to lose and I don't care because I just consider life a game." Yes, that's the way they are and you're delusional if you think you're going to change them. Here are a few examples, of many I could share from my life experience, as an example of this lesson. Bear in mind as you read this story that I was a young 28-year-old at the time of this life lesson.

I sold a business that I owned. I was not in a financially strong position at the time. The business had some debt obligations that had to be paid. I wanted out and to be free of these obligations and I was working 60 hours a week running two similar businesses in two different towns, which affected my mental well-being and especially my family's well-being. The business had gross sales of $2,800,000 and a gross profit of $420,000 a year. I sold the business on the basis that I was to receive 50 percent of the gross profits for five years, but the debt obligations were to be paid from my 50 percent of the gross profit. The buyer was to pay off the debt, which coincidentally had a five-year payoff. Everything seemed great to me. The business was stable, the normal attrition rate of customers and gross profit was 8 percent a year, so at the end of five years there should be $276,814 of gross profit left in the final year and I would get some money back for my time and trouble of putting the business together and running it myself for two years before selling it.

As the five years unfolded, a big surprise was in store for me! The new owner of my business merged my business in with theirs. They were in the same business I was in. They kept records of my business and presented me with gross figures of the income. I had no way to access individual customer records and see what happened to my old customers. The buy-sell contract that was drawn up made no provision for my ability to check their records. When I pressed the issue to check their records, I was told that the only way to check their records was to have their CPA firm check the records to track the history of my customers and determine what had happened to them and their contributing profit, at a cost of $75 per hour per person while working on the audit. I had proposed that two former employees of the business that worked for me check the records as they were familiar with the business, the customers and the management system that held all of the records and they were willing to accept $15 per hour to do this audit for me. It was not to be! The buyer insisted that the only party who could access their records was their local CPA firm that was going to charge me $150 an hour for their two associates to do the auditing of the records. These associates did not understand the nuances of the business, the management system that held all of the records and would spend countless hours looking for needles in the haystack due to their unfamiliarity of the business. They were accountants.

A wise attorney once told me that he always leaves $100 in the room and leaves the room to see if it's still there when he comes back when dealing with people in a business deal.

The kicker of this story is that in the fifth year of their ownership of my business, the gross profit had declined from $420,000 to $114,000. I sold the business and relieved myself of the debt it had, but I got $14,000 for the business in the end. I gave the business to them in a way. Do you think they knew how they were going to "take advantage" of me before they signed the contract to buy my business? You bet they did! I laid it all in the hands of God, who will judge us all in perfect judgment in the end and went on with my life, learning a great life lesson.

Interestingly enough, many years later a good friend of mine shared with me that he had sold his business at retirement and that he had sold it on the basis of the profits it made over the next five years. I said, "Sorry, you're going to get the pipe put to you." He asked me how I knew what had happened to him. I shared with him my story and he shared with me that the same thing had happened to him. The business declined rapidly and the new owners made little effort to keep his old customers. He had once had the best business of its kind in town. Today his business is a shadow of what it was the day he sold it. He gave his business away too, to greedy people playing the same game.

A wise attorney once told me that he always leaves $100 in the room and leaves the room to see if it's still there when he comes back when dealing with people in a business deal. I don't know exactly how he does this, but he always comes up with a way to check someone's honesty, integrity and intentions before he or his clients do business with them. Please remember this story before signing a contract with anyone to sell a business or to enter a business relationship with them. Leave some money out on the table and come back in the room and see if it's still there. See if their intent is honesty, integrity and fair dealing before doing business with them. Remember, "The Lord demands fairness in every business deal. He established this principle."

LIFE LESSON:
Greed is the most constant human emotion.

The Lord, Family and Forgiveness

By Gene "Coon" Hargis Sr.
Bledsoe County Regional Prison
Pikeville, Tenn.

*M*y name is Gene Hargis. I grew up in Battle Creek, which was not exactly considered the center of proper society in South Pittsburg, Tenn. I graduated from South Pittsburg High School in 1969. I was a leader on the football team. Graham Swafford tells me I had many good friends and many more who thought extremely well of me.

Early in life, I got married, obtained a job and had a beautiful child. I considered myself a hard-working fellow who loved his family.

> *... prior to my incarceration I was considered a stable, dependable, hard-working guy.*

In 1980, I was charged with a criminal offense for which I was ultimately convicted. I have spent the last 33 years incarcerated; however, prior to my incarceration I was considered a stable, dependable, hard-working guy.

After my incarceration, my son "Little Gene" was raised by David Payne and my sister, Mary Katherine Payne. My son has grown up to be a very successful person. He is currently a lead detective at the Marion County Sheriff's Department, has sat on the county commission for over 10 years and at one point was even the Interim County Mayor. Words cannot express the pride I have in my child. Words cannot express the gratitude for what David and Mary Katherine did. David and Mary Katherine could not have done any better.

As the years have come and gone, I have learned quite a few lessons. I have seen good and I have seen evil. I suppose, from my perspective, I could write a book myself, but I will just leave you with some of the greatest lessons I have learned:

Nothing is more important than forgiveness. Primarily, forgiveness comes from the Lord; however, it is incredibly important for individuals to forgive. Words cannot express the gratitude I have for the Lord's forgiveness and for the forgiveness I have received from my former wife's family.

The love, devotion and loyalty of your family means everything.

Don't judge a person by the color of their skin or what part of town they are from.

Don't be fooled by well-heeled members of proper society. We are all God's children.

The loyalty of a good friend can make all the difference.

There are those who do the work and there are those who get the glory. Don't forget the fellow who does the work.

Be careful about relationships.

Be loyal to friends.

Keep your business at home.

LIFE'S LESSON:

Nothing is more important than the Lord's forgiveness along with your family's forgiveness and their support.

---

*Note from Graham Swafford: I have known Gene "Coon" Hargis all my life. Coon will always be a good friend.

What I Learned at the University of Tennessee

By Graham Swafford

*I*n the fall of 1970, I entered the University of Tennessee to pursue my academic career. About all I can say is the University of Tennessee sure beat Vietnam. I only learned three things at the University of Tennessee — and nothing else! So the "Life's Lesson" I learned from my alma mater can be kept short and sweet.

LIFE'S LESSON:

What I learned at the University of Tennessee:

1. I met Sharon at the University of Tennessee and that made the experience all worthwhile;

2. I learned if you have an appetite for gambling, don't bet on the Vols. The Vols are both unpredictable and undependable;

3. I learned when someone tells you how rich they are — don't believe a word of it. This is typically code for "they're broke as hell."

Lesson 76

The Houses on the Hill

By Jerry B. Bible
Jasper, Tenn.

I have been fortunate that life's lessons were present in an almost continuing stream. I was raised by Bill and Hylis Bible, in a loving, nurturing, and supportive home where right and wrong and the recipe to be a productive person was emphasized and taught. Although I grew up in the church, I was saved and joined the church at the age of sixteen. Although over 40 years have passed, it seems like yesterday that my walk with my Lord began. Life's lessons have continually bombarded me while traveling to 50 of our states, most of Canada, parts of Mexico, and Europe. I have learned many things from these places and the people of these states, provinces, territories and countries.

I have reflected on and gained perspective on world events while visiting Fort Sumter where the Civil War began and Appomattox Court House where the Civil War ended. I have likewise visited Pearl Harbor where World War II for the United States began and walked on the deck of the U.S.S. Missouri where the documents that ended World War II were signed. I have stood where Hitler stood at Zeppelin Field, site of the Nuremberg Rallies. Here he enraged his countrymen to destroy mankind. I have visited Dachau Concentration Camp and seen the aftermath of his acts of inhumanity committed upon his fellow man. All of these events and others have moved me greatly and formed the person that I am today.

At "Jump School" (United States Parachute School), Ranger School, and various military schools up and through Command and General Staff College plus 21 years with the Tennessee Army National Guard, I learned about discipline and self-reliance. I could write a book on the life lessons learned from "Jump School" and Ranger School alone.

I have been moved by the lessons learned from my law practice and through the experiences of my clients through whom I have experienced a kaleidoscope of events.

All these and many others provided me with much enlightenment, but probably the greatest life lesson for me came when I had been in the National Guard for about six years and I wondered if I should leave the National Guard in order to devote more time to my wife and children. It so happened that at this time I was on a military assignment in Germany to reconnoiter locations for my field artillery battery in the event that a war erupted between the United States, NATO, and the Warsaw Pact. My trip had included travel to the then-East and -West German borders. At the small town of Heil in West Germany, I received a divisional briefing explaining how the division would defend against a possible attack by the East Germans and the Warsaw Pact. This area of Germany was part of the Fulda Gap, a large geographical corridor that had historically allowed large armies to pass through it quickly. It had been used by such armies as Napoleon's, the German's army, and any other large army since time eternal. Based on this history, it was anticipated that it would, likewise, be used by the Warsaw Pact to invade West Germany and Western Europe.

While in Heil, I was able to inspect the border between the two countries. I was able to look across the fortifications and barbed wire of the "Iron Curtain" and physically see the East German soldiers standing less than 50 yards away from me. I was also able to observe houses located inside the East German border. At first glance, at the houses, you did not notice that anything was wrong with the houses. The side of the houses, that was facing you, was neatly painted and appeared to be nicely kept. Upon further observation it was obvious that only the sides of these houses that faced west toward freedom were painted and not the sides that were less visible. The differences between East and West, communism and freedom, where I stood were striking. It was all about appearances to the East German Communists. It had nothing to do with the number of men in each army or the number of tanks, howitzers, or planes each had. Communism was a lie, a lie which they knew and accepted, otherwise, they would have painted the other sides of the houses. It was obvious on the communist side of those barbed wire fences what a lie the people on the other side were living. The contradictory appearance of the houses was almost an unspoken cry for help. The freedom that we often take for granted is such a rare commodity in our world.

I returned home after my trip to a country where we paint all sides of our homes and I resolved myself to complete my career with the National Guard. I was resolved to play my part, however small, with countless others serving in the military to stand against the dark forces that were present on the other side of the barbed wire. To my surprise, the Iron Curtain fell without the war we expected and feared. East and West Germany were reunited and the satellite countries of the Warsaw Pact became independent countries.

LIFE'S LESSON:

This life's lesson proved that the combined efforts of each like-minded individual can end tyranny, oppression, and replace them with freedom. Men and women should not have to live a lie.

Life's Lessons

By Nancy Rigsby
Jasper, Tenn.

LIFE'S LESSON:

My mother, Edna Ridge, taught me to know what you believe and why you believe it — not to take after every win and doctrine, which is biblical.

She also taught me to have the motto: Serve humanity and don't keep a record of what you do. Always give from the heart.

Always work hard every day and do the best you can do at whatever endeavor you're engaged. Then rest! If you don't wake up the next morning, then it won't matter anyway.

Flattery is like perfume, it smells good, but if you swallow it, it gets bitter!

Do what's right, even when nobody is watching you!

Anger is like taking poison and expecting the other person to die.

It costs nothing to dream but everything if you don't.

With every adversity, there's an equal or greater gift.

Life is made up of experiences — learn or do something new every day.

Cutting Corners or Being Cheap

By Graham Swafford

*T*he next life lesson I offer does not include a story but will make a point.
I have no criticism of somebody who considers themselves cheap or downright thrifty.

I learned a long time ago 99 percent of the world doesn't know the difference between a real Rolex and a fake Rolex. I know the Omega Watch Company advertises their watches were used by astronauts going to the moon; however, a $20 Timex can keep time just as well as the gold Omega Sea Master.

> *A $20 Timex can keep time just as well as the gold Omega Sea Master.*

I repeat — I am not unmindful of the fact that some people don't know the difference between an elevator with music and a high-end Mercedes Benz. A Hart, Shaffner and Marx suit bought at Goodwill is usually about as good as the Hart, Shaffner and Marx suit purchased at the most expensive department store. Most don't know the difference.

In my 35 years practicing law on the courthouse square in Jasper, Tenn., I learned there are three times when you don't cut corners:

1. Never cut corners on the roof you select and use for the house you build for yourself.

2. Never cut corners on the windows in the house in which you plan to live in yourself.

3. Never cut corners educating your children.

Without exception, when I or those I know have not followed the above advice, there has been regret, but when the above advice is followed, there has never been regret.

LIFE'S LESSON:

Be as cheap as you want, it does not make much difference. Most people don't know the difference between high class, low class or no class.

Never cut corners on the roof of your personal home, the windows of your personal home, or in educating your children.

A Day in the Life of an Assessor of Property

By Judy Brewer
Jasper, Tenn.

*W*hen Graham asked me to contribute a "Life's Lesson" for his book, this one automatically came to mind in my life as a property assessor.

I had only been in office about a year when a taxpayer, Mr. Albritton, sold off part of his property that resulted in rollback taxes (a penalty for use charge when on greenbelt). Well, you know taxes upset people anyway, especially when it is *additional* taxes. Mr. Albritton was really upset when he arrived at my office. We had a heated discussion about his rollback taxes and he proceeded to tell me I was a "crook," that I was not a nice person, and more. I told Mr. Albritton that I was a Christian woman and that I did not cheat anyone. He looked at me and said: "Well, you won't be long if you keep on doing people like you have done me."

Well, this really upset me! I slammed my hand down on my desk right in front of him and told him that no one, including him, was going to come between me and my God.

He looked me straight in the eyes and said "You know what I am fixing to do?" I had no idea what was about to happen. I said "No, sir, I don't." He said "I am going to Dairy Queen to get an ice cream." I didn't know what to say except: "I hope you enjoy it." He left my office without another word about his taxes.

Two weeks later, he called me and just wanted to know how I was. We had an enjoyable conversation. I never got to speak to Mr. Albritton again, because he died a short time later. I would have loved to have been able to have had another conversation with him. I truly believe he was a kind gentleman who was just having a bad day. We all have bad days, but it's best if we can not make it someone else's bad day too.

LIFE'S LESSON:

Stand up for your beliefs and always let people know God is first in your life and you never know when it will make a difference. I know Mr. Albritton respected me more for standing up to him than if I would have let him continue.

Edwin Z. Kelly Jr.

By Graham Swafford

For close to 35 years, I have practiced law on the courthouse square in Jasper, Tenn.

Our best competition came from Edwin Z. "Zack" Kelly Jr., and his cousin, Paul D. "Coon" Kelly.

Zack and Paul are the second most charming people I have ever met in my entire life.

Zack Kelly had a personal trait I found particularly annoying, but on reflection, might be considered a superior quality.

> *I am of the opinion that the ability to take secrets to the grave is not only an admirable quality, but a sign of character.*

About once every three months, for 35 years, Zack would give me a telephone call seeking advice. Generally, when a lawyer calls seeking advice from another, this is code for "wanting to know some gossip" or wants to "pump you for some facts."

For 30 years, every time Zack would call me seeking information (gossip), the flood gates would open. I would tell Zack everything I knew, everything I heard, not to mention everything I guessed. I guess I made up stuff to continue the enjoyment of talking to Zack.

Then, being the wise, old fox I thought I was, I would ask Zack to trade me a little information (gossip). Without exception, every time, Zack would then say he could not talk anymore because he had an appointment and/or he had to go to the bathroom and/or his wife, Elizabeth had just called his name and/or any excuse to get off the phone with me. *It happened every time.* In 35 years, I never received any good information (gossip) from Zack Kelly.

In my opinion, Zack Kelly and his cousin, Paul Kelly, will take more secrets to their graves than any two people on the planet. I am of the opinion that the ability to take secrets to the grave is not only an admirable quality, but a sign of character.

I don't give Zack any "information" anymore. Several years ago, Zack retired from the practice of law due to medical issues. His presence is missed on the courthouse square.

LIFE'S LESSON:

What I learned from Zack Kelly: Learning to keep your mouth shut and taking secrets to the grave is an admirable quality few enjoy.

Blessed Place

By Ronald Ramsey
Jasper, Tenn.

I remember coming to Jasper for the first time. The sheer beauty of going over Nickajack Reservoir was so amazing that we stopped in the rest area just to enjoy the sight. We were arriving to visit with the people of McKendree United Methodist Church as their new pastor and family.

It was April of 2009, I can remember the date so well because we visited McKendree on my daughter Rebecca's birthday.

We had visited Chattanooga the summer before to see the sights and go to the Chickamauga Battlefield for vacation. We discovered so many wonderful places and even got a view of Marion County when we rode the Tennessee Aquarium boat. One of the places we discovered was Sticky Finger's barbeque place and we went there to celebrate Rebecca's birthday.

Jasper welcomed us with a tornado. We sat in the hotel room watching the Weather Channel report on the storm that hit all around Marion County. The destruction wasn't bad but we did hear a young man was injured.

As we sat in the hotel room, we read the local papers and saw on the front of the Jasper Journal the story of Kennedy Griffith. There was a wonderful story about how bikers had raised a large amount of money to help the family. The article told about the many efforts of the community to help the family. As we went home we carried the newspapers with us and added Kennedy to our prayer list.

Over the months after we arrived we saw a community that surrounded Kennedy and her family with lots of love and support. There was a weekly reminder of her condition and needs through Amy Griffith, who was very active at McKendree. Amy kept the community up-to-date through her Caring Bridge reports and her kind spirit as she answered the same questions many times a day.

Rev. Cecil Baxter also would keep me up to date so that McKendree could pray for Kennedy and her family. Even after he retired, I could still get information from Rev. Baxter.

McKendree was involved in Relay for Life and so we jumped in. The church's team raised money and made popcorn and sold sodas during the walk. It was always a blessing to hear all the stories of the survivors and to celebrate the birthdays!

At every church and community gathering I heard prayers and support for

Kennedy and her family. I do not believe that there is a church in the community that doesn't pray for Kennedy and her family. We would update each other seeing who had the latest information.

From birthday parties for Kennedy to a huge crowd to hear her speak at Relay for Life, Marion County reached out over and over again to encourage and bless Kennedy. When she earned an honor everyone celebrated for they knew that the "warrior" deserved it.

By seeing the pain of others we see beyond ourselves and are able to seek help from a greater source, namely God.

I have been many places during my life and have seen many wonderful people and lived in good communities. Jasper and Marion County have much to be proud of! Their kindness and love for a young person suffering so much is not just seen in this one person though. I have seen efforts for many other young people suffering from cancer, or many others illnesses. At McKendree we have several children constantly on our prayer list and we seek to be updated so that our prayers can reach out to their needs and the needs of their families.

But Kennedy and the other children aren't just blessed — they are a blessing! They strengthen and bless the churches and community by bringing us together by sharing in their pain and concern. They keep us from centering on ourselves and becoming ingrained and indrawn. By seeing the pain of others we see beyond ourselves and are able to seek help from a greater source, namely God.

We become better Christians making better churches and a better community. For that is how growth and blessing should flow! It is so easy to see God's great blessings flow throughout the churches and the communities in Marion County.

LIFE'S LESSON:

As we see God's faithfulness to others who are suffering or in need, our faith is strengthened and we are drawn closer to God. We become able to pray for bigger things and for deeper things as we see God do great things in the lives of those for whom we pray. We become better Christians, church members, family members, and members of our community and our world.

Now we see the truth behind the declaration: "Praise God from whom all blessings flow!"

Remembering My Friend Kemper Durand

By Bill Haltom
Memphis, Tenn.

I lost a law partner and dear friend, Kemper Durand. Kemper left this earth the way I hope to when my time comes. He was seated in his favorite chair, by a fire, reading a good book. He closed his eyes, fell asleep and did not awaken.

Kemper was one of those extraordinary souls who always exuded joy and happiness, even in stressful times.

> **Kemper was one of those extraordinary souls who always exuded joy and happiness, even in stressful times.**

He enjoyed life immensely and lived it with intensity. He adored his wife, Lillian, his sons Jennings and Bartlett, and his grandchildren.

He also loved the Green Bay Packers, the Memphis Grizzlies, the Sunday New York Times, bird-watching, jazz, chicory coffee, and lunches with friends at his favorite restaurant the Little Tea Shop.

And, of course, he loved the law. He was a criminal defense lawyer and proud of it. He was a fan of John Mortimer's fictional British Barrister, Horace Rumpole. In the PBS television series, Rumpole of the Bailey (which Kemper enjoyed immensely), Rumpole would defend all sorts and conditions, including rich businessmen charged with fraud or poor street folks charged with petty crimes. Some were innocent, and some were guilty as sin, but Rumpole delighted in being the voice for them all.

Kemper was an American Rumpole of the Bailey. He delighted in being an advocate for unattractive people and unpopular causes.

Kemper was a tenacious advocate. But he was unfailingly professional and civil. In an era when the law is plagued by too many mean-spirited litigators, Kemper never took a cheap shot at opposing counsel. He was always the consummate professional, and accordingly, judges and juries loved him.

Former Federal Prosecutor Tim Dicenza said of him, "We were adversaries in the courtroom, and allies outside the court."

There are many stories to share about this remarkable man and his wonderful life, but for me, three illustrate the type of lawyer and man that he was.

The first involved Kemper's defense of an innocent man, Clark McMillan. For over 22 years, Mr. McMillan resided in a Tennessee prison, serving a sentence for the hideous crime of rape. Clark McMillan kept telling anyone who would listen to him that he was an innocent man. The problem, of course, was that no one would listen to him. But through something called the "Innocence Project," Clark McMillan found a lawyer...a lawyer named Kemper Durand.

Kemper listened to Clark McMillan. He listened, and he believed him. And Kemper not only listened to Clark McMillan. He took him on as a pro bono client. Kemper worked for months on behalf of his client. Finally, Kemper found the DNA evidence that proved Clark McMillan had never committed the crime for which he had been convicted. Kemper had the conviction set aside, and on a warm spring day, Clark McMillan walked out of prison, a free man...with his friend and lawyer, Kemper Durand, at his side.

The second story involves two young men who, unlike Clark McMillan, were not innocent. They were guilty of the crime of accosting and kidnapping a man. And that man, was Kemper.

One night several years ago, Kemper was leaving his office to head for home. As he was about to get in his car, he was accosted by two men, one of whom held a gun at Kemper's face and demanded his car keys. Kemper handed the keys over, and then at gunpoint, he was forced inside the trunk of his car.

It was a rare case in which the victim became the advocate for one of his assailants.

For the next several hours, Kemper was trapped in the cold darkness of his car trunk as the two men drove the car throughout the city. From time to time, the car would stop. The men would open the trunk, pull Kemper out, make him withdraw money from an ATM machine, and hand it over.

After several hours of this ordeal, Kemper was standing at gun point alongside yet another ATM machine when he noticed a security guard. Kemper yelled for help. His assailants fled, but were captured and arrested.

Both men were tried and found guilty. At the sentencing hearing for one of the two men, a well-known lawyer appeared in the courtroom. It was Kemper. He told the judge he wanted to testify. Kemper took the stand, and testified that the man who was about to be sentenced was not the man who accosted him at gun point on that fateful evening. Yes, the man had been there and could certainly be considered an accomplice, but as Kemper saw it, the man was at the wrong place with the wrong person at the wrong time. Kemper then further described how during those hours he spent in the trunk of his car, he heard the two men talking. The man who was now about to be sentenced had pleaded with his friend to "stop the car, let this man out, give him his keys, and go!"

Forever the effective criminal defense lawyer, Kemper portrayed the man before the judge as an unwilling accomplice. He asked that the judge give him the most lenient sentence possible. The judge agreed.

It was a rare case in which the victim became the advocate for one of his assailants.

> *He delighted in being an advocate for unattractive people and unpopular causes.*

The final story is about one of Kemper's many acts of kindness. One day not long ago, Kemper and I were headed to lunch at the Little Tea Shop. We were approached by a homeless man who asked us if we could "help (him) get something to eat."

I was ready to direct him to Calvary Church or the Memphis Union Mission. And then I heard Kemper's wonderful voice proclaim, "Sir, your timing is impeccable! My colleague, Mr. Haltom, and I are about to enjoy a wonderful lunch here at the Little Tea Shop. Would you please join us?"

The homeless man looked startled by Kemper's hospitality. He hesitated for a moment and then mumbled, "I guess so."

Kemper then escorted the homeless man and me through the doors of the Little Tea Shop. A few of the patrons glanced at the homeless man and no doubt wondered how he had stumbled into a restaurant frequented every day by judges, lawyers, and successful business people. But all the regulars at the Little Tea Shop knew Kemper, and they quickly realized that the homeless man was Kemper's guest.

The three of us were seated. Kemper assisted the homeless man in ordering his lunch. A wonderful meal was soon delivered, and the three of us broke bread together. Kemper tried to engage the homeless man in conversation. The man was obviously hungry and did not say much. But Kemper talked with him and treated him as if they were old classmates from Yale.

That day, Kemper did not just give the homeless man a nice lunch. He gave him dignity. He gave him respect.

Kemper treated all of us that way, whether we were his fellow lawyers, friends, clients or a homeless man he met on the street.

LIFE'S LESSON:

Kemper Durand set a good example — whether we were innocent, guilty, or a little bit of both, Kemper always gave each of us respect, kindness and grace.

Life Ain't Fair — Get Over It
or
A Life Lesson From My Dad

By Judge Tommy Moore
Dresden, Tenn.

I grew up in small town, Dresden, Tenn. My mother and dad were both teachers. My mother taught fourth grade. My dad taught math and was the assistant principal. My dad was also a disabled veteran and war hero, having lost both of his legs in a land mine explosion in World War II.

The families of my parents were incredibly poor. Adding to that poverty was the fact that both grew up in the midst of the Great Depression. My dad was orphaned about the age of 15. Despite the circumstances of their lives and the lack of privilege, both of my parents saw the importance of education and obtained college degrees.

As you might imagine, during my academic career I was the recipient of several of these triple whippings.

In our town, everyone knew each other. But that comment doesn't adequately describe the extent of information each of us acquired about the others in our community. We were more informed about each person; their backgrounds, life stories, family histories, genealogies and consanguinity to others in the area, than Ancestry.com or the Tennessee Bureau of Investigation.

Along with sports, hunting, fishing, politics and religion, other people were the subjects of our daily conversation and entertainment. By the time I was six, I knew everyone in the town, especially the teachers. So that is why I was confused when, on the first day of each new school year, my Dad accompanied me to class and introduced me to my teacher, a person I had known since birth.

The introduction to this educator was very formal. My dad would say, "Ms. Alexander, this is my son Tommy. Tommy this is Ms. Alexander, your new teacher." Then he issued an edict, every year, I dreaded hearing, and during the delivery of which I cringed. "Ms. Alexander, if you have to whip him, just let me know and then he'll get a whipping from his mother and a whipping from me and then we will ask him why he got a whipping." Even at six, I comprehended that proviso.

As you might imagine, during my academic career I was the recipient of several of these triple whippings. There were a few times when the teacher took pity and my classmates kept the code of silence and my parents remained ignorant of the corporal punishment episode. But the norm was that I assumed the position three times for every delinquent or mischievous act. I came to be resigned, to accept this Draconian sanction as my lot in life.

Then one day, when I was 12 years of age, I was improperly accused, tried, convicted, and punished — though my innocence was vehemently argued. Home was not a sanctuary for the guiltless. There I was paddled twice. Then I sat on the ottoman in front of my Dad's easy chair and shared my tale of injustice.

I probably already knew life wasn't fair, but that day solidified it in my mind and I never worried about it after that.

My Dad had no legal training, but immediately perceived that I had been wronged. He said, "You shouldn't have gotten a whipping that time, son." I responded, "I shouldn't have gotten three whippings." He shrugged his assent and I continued. "What are you going to do about it?" He interjected, "What do you mean?" I explained, "I mean, are you going to go talk to that teacher and the principal and plead my case — make them at least apologize and admit that I was not in the wrong? Are you going to defend my honor and reputation?"

Then he asked me, "How many times you figure that you didn't get a whipping when you should've got a whipping?" I answered, "Hundreds." That is when he shared a piece of wisdom, a jewel of knowledge with me. He philosophized, "I ain't gonna do nothing. Life ain't fair — get over it! Now get out of the way, so I can watch TV."

I was actually stunned and disappointed — for a moment. Then in a matter of seconds, I looked at him and reflected and pondered about his life. Both legs blown off. Had to work his way through school. Grew up poor. Orphaned at 15 years of age. Wearing heavy wooden legs. Suffering from diabetes and the shingles. In pain most of each day. Middle class at best.

As I remember it today, I got up and walked away from him a couple of steps, with my back to him. Then I turned and said, "OK." I recall that he and I both kind of grinned in our show of understanding and agreement. I knew he was right. I probably already knew life wasn't fair, but that day solidified it in my mind and I never worried about it after that. It was a watershed day for me. It was one of those days I often fondly reflect on.

Life really wasn't fair for me either, but I knew that because of my mother and father, it was easier for me than for them. I was short and skinny, of average intelligence, with little athletic skill, not a person that stood out in a crowd of class mates. So I realized, because I had not been blessed with looks, genius, height, and skill, that I had to study, work, scrap, entertain and practice to stick out. I did not become bitter, ever. I never worried about it. I never developed a chip on my shoulder about life. Today I have few complaints and many praises and blessings.

LIFE LESSON:

Life ain't fair — get over it.

Final comment: My dad adeptly taught me in a few minutes of conversation, but more with a life time of example, that we shouldn't let the circumstances of our life change us into a bitter or disappointed person. We should rise above our inadequacies and disabilities. We should remember, never forget, the times in our lives when we are mistreated and experience injustice, yet often the best course of action is to walk away, without retaliation, using the experience to become people who fight for justice, equality and fairness.

What I Learned From Helen Brooks or the Gift

By Stephen Hargis
Chattanooga, Tenn.

*G*rowing up in the country, removed from many of my friends who lived in town, I had to find creative ways to entertain myself as a kid. Mostly that included spending my afternoons playing outside in our yard, mimicking my sports heroes, whether it was making buzzer-beating jump-shots on the basketball court my dad had made for me, or diving over hedges, pretending they were tacklers, with a football under my arm, I developed a pretty healthy imagination, and many of my daydreams revolved around sports.

Find something you like doing, find somebody who will pay you to do it, and you'll never feel like you're working a day in your life.

I put my imagination to good use during Mrs. Helen Brooks' 7th and 8th grade English composition classes. Writing was something that just came easily to me and I soon found myself writing more than the required one composition a week, making up and telling stories and learning to appreciate the way my classmates enjoyed my tales. From early on, Mrs. Brooks encouraged me to practice writing, even if it was just to keep a journal for myself, because she believed I had a talent for it.

Unfortunately, genetics determined that I would be a late bloomer and throughout my high school days, I was well under 6-feet tall and barely 125 pounds soaking wet. I decided to try football anyway, but as a scrawny freshman, it took all of two days, and one dizzying hit by a former South Pittsburg all-state linebacker, to realize I probably needed to find another sport.

I knew I was making the right decision when I went in to tell Coach Don Grider I had decided to wait another year, see if I grew and then try it again and Coach Grider's response was simply, "That's probably a good idea."

So for the next couple of years I ran track, played basketball and waited to grow. The growth spurt never happened, but my love of sports and my desire to be around the games never lessened and by the time I started college, my freshman advisor gave me the greatest piece of advice I could hope for.

"Find something you like doing, find somebody who will pay you to do it, and you'll never feel like you're working a day in your life." Suddenly I remembered

Mrs. Brooks' encouragement and decided I would combine my love of sports and the God-given talent I had to write. I majored in communications, was able to earn a part-time job at the Chattanooga News-Free Press during my second semester in college and soon was getting paid to watch and tell the story ballgames. It didn't take long before I was hooked and, sure enough, because I had found something I truly enjoyed doing, I've traveled throughout the Southeast, telling the stories of both famous and little-known athletes. And while I never grew into an athlete myself, I've been blessed in that never once have I felt like I've had to work a day in my life.

LIFE'S LESSON:

What I was taught by Helen Brooks: Find what you love doing and make it your life's work.

Our Story

By Ruth Swafford O'Leary
South Pittsburg, Tenn.

*O*n May 28, 1949, I married my high school sweetheart, Bill O'Leary. We were married for 52 years and had five children: Dean (married to Sheila Siler); Allen, Beth (Jim) Webb; Dan (Candy Curtis) and Mark (Misty Daffron). Bill was a person of such integrity that I never once wondered where he was and who he was with and what he was doing. We were "in love" until the day he died in 2002. I thought I would never love again.

Bill worked for BellSouth Telephone Co. and I taught piano. We lived in Chattanooga, Nashville, Knoxville, Memphis and New Orleans. After moving around for 27 years, we finally came back home to South Pittsburg, Tenn., in 1976.

I thought I would never love again.

At First Baptist Church in South Pittsburg, where Bill was a deacon and Sunday School teacher, we were good friends with Leonard and Jo (Boyd) Wynne. He, too, was a deacon and in Bill's Sunday School class. He sang in the choir with me. We have been friends all our lives and Jo was his high school sweetheart. Leonard was with Coca-Cola for 50 years. (You couldn't hold a gun to his head and make him drink a Pepsi).

Jo developed Alzheimer's when she was in her sixties. Leonard lovingly cared for her for almost 10 years. The last few years she didn't even know him. They were happily married for 54 years and had two children: Susan and Jerry (Jerry is married to Cammy Hudson). Jo died in 2004 and Leonard thought he would never love again.

On the day before Thanksgiving 2005, my granddaughter, Erin O'Leary, was having an operation on her tongue and Leonard came to the hospital to be with the family. We went out to eat together. Following that, Leonard would call every few days, and I would think up some excuse to call him (or was it the other way around?) Never mind — our relationship blossomed and we have been "courting" for six years.

Neither one of us wanted to get married. At our age it just complicates life — mixing families and finances. Besides, I like to live in my house and he likes to live in his (his basement would drive me crazy). We both like to do our own thing and just "run around" together. We both still wear our wedding rings and people assume we are married. We will go out to eat and the waitress will ask us: "How long have you been married?" Leonard will always reply: "106 years." Then we have to explain that we aren't married — we're just sweethearts.

LIFE'S LESSONS:

1. You are never too old to love (I am 84 and Leonard is 81).

2. Be happy — keep enjoying life until the day you die.

3. A happy marriage is built on love and complete trust in each other.

4. You are happiest if faith in God is a vital part of your relationship.

5. Marriage is not always the best option the second time around. (Maybe you should just "jump over the broom.")

September 1935

By Graham Swafford

The Road Not Taken
Two roads diverged in a yellow wood
And sorry I could not travel both
And be one traveler, long I stood
And looked down one as far as I could
To where it bent in the undergrowth;
Then took the other, as just as far
And having perhaps the better claim,
Because it was grassy and wanted wear;
Though as for that, the passing there
Had worn them really about the same,
And both that morning equally lay
In leaves no step had trodden back.
Oh, I kept the first for another day!
Yet knowing how way leads on to way,
I doubted if I should ever come back.
I shall be telling with a sigh
Somewhere ages and ages hence:
Two roads diverged in a wood and I —
I took the one less traveled by,
And that has made all the difference.

— *Robert Frost*

I will conclude my book with a very personal story which represents an expression of gratitude from my sister and me, along with our families.

Without a doubt, this story and/or "life lesson" represents a turning point if not one of the most important moments in our lives.

I want to state this "life lesson" up front, which I believe *beyond a shadow of a doubt:*

Individual decisions made by individuals at any level can make a difference that will effect generations.

So here are the facts: In 1935, my father was 16 years old. Growing up had not been easy in South Pittsburg, Tenn. America was in the Great Depression. My grandmother, Ida Graham Swafford, had literally kept the family together through the force of will and character along with the First Baptist Church of South Pittsburg, Tenn.

In September 1935, at the age of 16, my father walked to the edge of South Pittsburg, Tenn., carrying all his worldly possessions and hitch-hiked to the University of Tennessee in Knoxville, with only $75 in his pocket which he had accumulated working for Edith Lodge Kellerman.

My sister Claudia and I have never let a day pass that we do not recognize that on that day at that moment with that individual decision by that 16-year-old boy, with that $75, the world changed for this family (and particularly my sister and I) on a dime!

Fast forward 35 years. At a time when many young men of my age were packed off for the Vietnam adventure, I drove to the University of Tennessee in an Oldsmobile 442 to pursue my academic pursuits. It might be a great surprise to my readers, but it never crossed my mind or my sister's mind to apply for an academic scholarship (if you know what I mean.)

My sister and I both graduated from college and law school without owing a dime, the education all having been willingly financed by our parents.

Although my sister and I have, at times, been considered entertaining if not capable, we both acknowledge good things have been lavished upon us that had absolutely nothing to do with our individual merit. My sister and I benefited because of the good fortune of to whom we were born. Clearly, where we landed was just the luck of the draw.

My sister went on to Memphis where she became a judge and by all accounts has done pretty well, not to mention she became an Episcopalian and a Democrat (a fact I mention for academic integrity).

The greatest monument to my parents is the fact that notwithstanding the fact our family seems to have an opinion on everything in the world and an irrepressible urge to voice our opinions on matters which we have no knowledge, my sister, Claudia, and I have never had a hateful conversation.

Although Claudia and I would like to take personal credit (which we both acknowledge we readily deserve) for our many fine qualities and accomplishments, we acknowledge these qualities were acquired from our parents.

LIFE'S LESSON:

At certain times, individuals make singular decisions that make all the difference in the world. Countless generations are effected for good or for bad.

My sister and I, along with our families, have enjoyed drinking from many wells we did not dig. We convey an expression of gratitude to our parents

The author's father, Howard Graham Swafford, Naval Aviator in WWII.

UNITED STATES PACIFIC FLEET

COMMANDER BATTLESHIP SQUADRON TWO

In the name of the President of the United States, the Commander Battleship Squadron TWO, Pacific Fleet, presents the AIR MEDAL to

ENSIGN HOWARD GRAHAM SWAFFORD
UNITED STATES NAVAL RESERVE

for service as set forth in the following

CITATION:

"For distinguishing himself by meritorious acts while partici-
pating in aerial flights in operations against the enemy held Nansei
Shoto during the period 1 March to 19 April 1945. As pilot of a
battleship-based observation plane on 1 March 1945 while on a successful air-sea rescue mission to within gun range of a strongly held
enemy island and again during March and April 1945 in spotting flights
over an enemy held island during Naval gunfire, he skillfully per-
formed his assigned duties thereby bringing accurate fire on enemy
positions. His devotion to duty and courage were in keeping with the
highest traditions of the United States Naval Service".

W.A. Lee, jr.,
Vice Admiral, U.S.Navy.